Romans

Westminster Bible Companion

Series Editors

Patrick D. Miller
David L. Bartlett

Romans

DAVID L. BARTLETT

 Westminster John Knox Press
Louisville, Kentucky

Book design by Publishers' WorkGroup
Cover design by Drew Stevens

First edition

Published by Westminster John Knox Press
Louisville, Kentucky

This book is printed on acid-free paper that meets the American National Standards Institute Z39.48 standard. ♾

PRINTED IN THE UNITED STATES OF AMERICA

95 96 97 98 99 00 01 02 03 04 — 10 9 8 7 6 5 4 3 2 1

Library of Congress Cataloging-in-Publication Data

Bartlett, David Lyon
    Romans / David L. Bartlett. — 1st ed.
       p.   cm. — (Westminster Bible companion)
    ISBN 0-664-25254-0 (alk. paper)
    1. Bible. N.T. Romans—Commentaries. I. Title. II. Series.
BS2665.3.B344 1995
227'.1077—dc20
                                       95-10453

Contents

Series Foreword

This series of study guides to the Bible is offered to the church and more specifically to the laity. In daily devotions, in church school classes, and in listening to the preached word, individual Christians turn to the Bible for a sustaining word, a challenging word, and a sense of direction. The word that scripture brings may be highly personal as one deals with the demands and surprises, the joys and sorrows, of daily life. It also may have broader dimensions as people wrestle with moral and theological issues that involve us all. In every congregation and denomination, controversies arise that send ministry and laity alike back to the Word of God to find direction for dealing with difficult matters that confront us.

A significant number of lay women and men in the church also find themselves called to the service of teaching. Most of the time they will be teaching the Bible. In many churches, the primary sustained attention to the Bible and the discovery of its riches for our lives have come from the ongoing teaching of the Bible by persons who have not engaged in formal theological education. They have been willing, and often eager, to study the Bible in order to help others drink from its living water.

This volume is part of a series of books, the Westminster Bible Companion, intended to help the laity of the church read the Bible more clearly and intelligently. Whether such reading is for personal direction or for the teaching of others, the reader cannot avoid the difficulties of trying to understand these words from long ago. The scriptures are clear and clearly available to everyone as they call us to faith in the God who is revealed in Jesus Christ and as they offer to every human being the word of salvation. No companion volumes are necessary in order to hear such words truly. Yet every reader of scripture who pauses to ponder and think further about any text has questions that are not immediately answerable simply by reading the text of scripture. Such questions may be about historical and geographical details or about words that are obscure or so loaded with meaning that one cannot tell at a glance what is at stake. They may be about the fundamental meaning of a passage or about what connection a particular text might have to our contemporary world. Or a teacher preparing for a church school class may simply want to know: What should I say about this biblical passage when I have to teach it next Sunday? It is our hope that these volumes, written by teachers and pastors with long experience studying and teaching the Bible in the church, will help members of the church who want and need to study the Bible with their questions.

The New Revised Standard Version of the Bible is the basis for the interpretive comments that each author provides. The NRSV text is presented at the beginning of the discussion so that the reader may have at hand in a single volume both the scripture passage and the exposition of its meaning. In some instances, where inclusion of the entire passage is not necessary for understanding either the text or the interpreter's discussion, the presentation of the NRSV text may be abbreviated. Usually, the whole of the biblical text is given.

We hope this series will serve the community of faith, opening the Word of God to all the people, so that they may be sustained and guided by it.

Introduction
Paul Introduces Himself

From time to time we get letters of introduction. A friend of a friend writes to say that she will be in town next week and would like to meet us. Perhaps she has interests that she shares with us. She is eager to see the local sites or learn about our region's history. Or a distant relative writes to say that he has childhood memories of our father and would like to stop by and chat. We got a letter once from the niece of the man who had owned our home before we did and who had died some years earlier. The niece didn't know us, but she knew our house and had warm memories of it. Could she stop by and introduce herself?

Romans is Paul's letter of introduction.

When Paul wrote his letter to the Romans, he wrote to a group of churches he did not found and had not yet visited. All other letters of Paul's that we possess were written to churches Paul had founded or to a person he knew well. In this letter Paul introduces himself and the gospel he proclaims to strangers. With a few exceptions, the Roman Christians know him only by reputation, and they know his gospel only by rumor. He wants them to know him better, and he has information, good news, that he is eager to share.

Paul writes the letter to the Roman Christians for at least three reasons. First, he introduces himself to them in the hope that before long he will be able to visit them in person, as he travels on to bring the gospel to Spain (see Rom. 1:8–14; 15:22–29). In the first century, even more so than in our time of telephone and E-mail, a letter was the next best thing to being there. Paul writes because he cannot yet visit. He writes because he hopes to visit Rome soon.

Second, Paul writes to enlist the prayers of the Roman congregations for his upcoming visit to Jerusalem. One of the great goals of Paul's ministry was to bring an offering from the Gentile (non-Jewish) churches to the poor people of the churches in Jerusalem. The leaders of Christianity in Jerusalem, including Peter and John, Jesus' early followers, have ac-

knowledged Paul as a missionary to the Gentiles. At the same time they
have asked him to help meet the needs of the Jerusalem community (see
Gal. 2:1–10). The concern among these early leaders for the poor in
Jerusalem undoubtedly represented a response to a real need for material
help. More than that, however, for Paul the offering had become a sign of
the unity of the whole church. Gentiles are being asked to help Jews because all are part of the family of God. Paul asks the prayers of the Roman
Christians as he sets out on his trip to Jerusalem:

> I appeal to you, brothers and sisters, by our Lord Jesus Christ and by the
> love of the Spirit, to join me in earnest prayer to God on my behalf, that I
> may be rescued from the unbelievers in Judea, and that my ministry to
> Jerusalem may be acceptable to the saints, so that by God's will I may come
> to you with joy and be refreshed in your company. (Rom. 15:30–32)

The third reason Paul writes to the Romans is that he has some knowledge of their situation. Some time before Paul writes this letter, a Christian community had begun in Rome. The Christian community consisted
of a number of house churches, congregations that met in the home of one
of the Christian families.

The early Christian community included both house churches whose
members were mostly Jewish and house churches whose members were
mostly Gentile. A number of Jewish Christians, like Priscilla and Aquila,
came to faith in Christ after growing up as members of the synagogue.
However, in A.D. 49, a few years before Paul wrote Romans, the emperor
Claudius forced Jewish people, including Jewish Christians, to leave
Rome. Apparently he expelled the Jews because he was disturbed by the
possibility that Jews who believed in Christ might cause trouble in the city.
(See Acts 18:1–2. The Roman writer Suetonius also refers to Claudius's
banning of the Jews.)

When the Jewish Christians were forced to leave Rome, Gentile Christians, meeting in their own house churches, made up virtually all of the
congregations. Gentile practices prevailed in worship, organization, and
even in something as basic as the menus shared at common meals. In some
ways Gentile Christians were different from Jewish Christians. They
were, for example, freer in their interpretation of the Old Testament and
less concerned with strict rules for their diet.

When Paul writes Romans, Claudius has died. His edict against Jews
has been lifted by his successor, Nero (in A.D. 54). Jewish Christians are
returning to Rome. Paul knows some of these Jewish Christians, like

Priscilla and Aquila. He is concerned that when they return to the church, the church will find a place for all believers—Gentiles and Jews alike. Paul sums up this concern in Romans 15:7: "Welcome one another, therefore, just as Christ has welcomed you, for the glory of God."

For at least these reasons, Paul writes his letter to the church at Rome. The letter is full of Paul's passion for the gospel of Jesus Christ. For him, and he believes for all humankind, Jesus is the one in whom God turns human history around, doing what is right for the Roman Christians and for the whole creation.

ONE GOD: ONE PEOPLE

The claim that in Jesus Christ God does what is right for the whole creation is at the heart of the letter to the Christians at Rome. The claim that God is God of all people and of all the universe speaks to each of the concerns that caused Paul to write his letter.

The claim that God is God of all is at the heart of the gospel Paul preaches. It is the good news he wants to confirm in the hearts of the Roman Christians. In introducing himself, Paul needs to introduce this gospel.

The claim that God is God of all helps explain Paul's ministry. Paul, a Jew, is an apostle to Gentiles. As a sign of the unity of all people under one God, Paul hopes to bring the offering to Jerusalem. He asks for the prayers and support of the Roman Christians.

The claim that God is God of all provides Paul with his arguments for hospitality and fellowship on the part of the Roman Christians. Gentile Christians should welcome Jewish Christians back to the church, because in Jesus Christ the same God reaches out to embrace Jews and Gentiles alike. "Welcome one another, just as Christ has welcomed you."

The central claim of Romans therefore is this: there is one God, who in the one person Jesus Christ chooses redemption for all people—and for the whole creation. Paul writes Romans to affirm and expand the central claim of his Jewish tradition: the Lord God is one. In making this claim, Paul picks up one strain of the Hebrew scripture. God is not only the God of Israel but the God of all peoples. If God is not the God of all peoples, God is not really God but someone smaller, a half god, a mini-god.

So Paul writes: ". . . is God the God of Jews only? Is he not the God of Gentiles also? Yes, of Gentiles also, since God is one; and he will justify the circumcised on the ground of faith and the uncircumcised through that same faith" (Rom. 3:29–30).

We notice something here we need to examine further: because God is one God, all people are invited to receive the one God in one way—through faith.

In Romans 10 Paul is discussing the ways in which God works to redeem both Jews and Gentiles, both Israel and the pagan world. He quotes Isaiah 28:16 and then goes on to explain:

> The scripture says, "No one who believes [has faith] in him will be put to shame." For there is no distinction between Jew and Greek; the same Lord is Lord of all and is generous to all who call on him. For, "Everyone who calls on the name of the Lord shall be saved." (Rom. 10:11–13)

In this second quotation, from Joel 2:32, Paul suggests that faith consists partly in calling on the name of the Lord. Again his fundamental claim is that because the Lord is one, there is one way for all people to receive God's goodness—through faith.

As he comes to the conclusion of his discussion of the relationship of Israel and the Gentiles in God's plan, Paul breaks into a kind of hymn that affirms the oneness of God, the God of all peoples and of all creation.

> O the depth of the riches and wisdom and knowledge of God! How unsearchable are his judgments and how inscrutable his ways!
> "For who has known the mind of the Lord?
>   Or who has been his counselor?"
> "Or who has given a gift to him,
>   to receive a gift in return?"
> For from him and through him and to him are all things. To him be the glory forever. Amen. (Rom. 11:33–36)

Again Paul has quoted scripture to make his point (Isa. 40:13; Job 35:7; 41:11).

Now we can sum up three claims that are at the heart of Romans:

1. God is God of every human, of human history, and of all creation. God is one.
2. The one God has determined a way by which to stake God's claim over all people, through the cross and resurrection of Jesus Christ. Christ is God's gift, not just for one group but for all of humankind.
3. The way in which all of humankind—of whatever nationality or religion—can acknowledge God's claim is through faith in the one person Jesus Christ.

It may seem at first glance that Paul is writing for a time far different from our own. Yet even today the claim that there is one God who deals with all of humankind through the one person Jesus Christ cuts against much of our popular understanding.

The divisiveness within the church of Christ, sometimes polite, sometimes angry, can reflect the assumption that the one God has chosen to be God only of one chosen group of Christian believers.

Sometimes the chosen are supposed to be marked by their denominational allegiance. Only members of a particular Baptist denomination or a particular Presbyterian group or a particular congregation of Pentecostal Christians are God's own people.

In other instances the chosen are marked by their ethical behavior. Only those who refuse all alcohol or tobacco, or only those who support a particular policy on gun control, or only those who dress in a particular way are God's people.

Finally, the chosen may be marked by their piety or their theology. Only those who have the gift of speaking in tongues are God's chosen people. (Or, for others, those who have the gift of speaking in tongues are deluded and not a legitimate group within the church.) Only those who believe in biblical inerrancy have the right to call themselves Christians. These alone are the people God has chosen.

Those who claim to believe in the one God, but say that the one God is the God of inerrantists or Free Methodists or teetotalers only, do not believe in Paul's God. The God who is God is not the God of Gentiles only, or of Jews only, or of Southern Baptists only, or of charismatics only. Such a God would be not God but a demigod, not really worthy of our worship or devotion. The God who is God chooses to be God of all faithful people.

Faith, for Paul, is not a matter of getting your doctrine on biblical inspiration right, or of refusing to smoke, or even of voting for the right political candidate. Faith is loyalty to the one God who is God of all people. God's intention to be God of all people is demonstrated in Jesus Christ.

There is also a harder question. Is God the God of Christians only? Romans pushes us to stretch our understanding of the range of God's mercy. The great struggle of Romans 9—11 shows Paul's attempt to prove that God must be God of Gentile and Jewish Christians but also, still, the God of Israel. In our time even larger questions are raised. Is not God the God of Muslims and Buddhists and Hindus, too? At the very least we must say that though it may be true that it is only through faith that people acknowledge God, we do not want to say that God acknowledges only faithful people. We affirm that in Jesus Christ Christian people know a fundamental truth about the one true God. Yet the fundamental truth we know includes the acknowledgment that the one true God is not only the God of Christian people. There can be no such thing as a "Christian God" but only the one true God in whom we Christians place our trust.

Not only do many today believe in a kind of tribal god, the god of one people only, many today still believe in many gods. We have our own version of the paganism from which the Gentile Christians of Rome had been converted. Of course our belief in many gods may be implicit and hidden, but it is there.

Atheism (the belief that there is no God) and agnosticism (leaving the question of God open) are intellectual positions for which people argue with integrity. Yet because they are human, even people who are atheists or agnostics do not live without faith. No one can get through the day, or through the hazards and hopes of life, or through the crises of history, without having some loyalties. It may well be that people who do not believe in God do not have a single focus for their loyalty, or what the theologian Paul Tillich called an "ultimate concern." All of us, however, have loyalties, allegiances. Our temptation today, as in the first century, is to trust a multitude of middle-sized gods.

Our supposedly secular culture is full of people who have faith in the scientific method, in the powers of their own intellect, in the virtues of self-fulfillment, in their family, in the democratic process, in America, in success. What many people do not believe is that there is one ultimate source and goal of loyalty—the God revealed in Jesus Christ. Paul would say that that God, the true God, judges and completes all our other loyalties. Paul says of God that "from him and through him and to him are all things" (Rom. 11:36). That claim is as odd in twentieth-century Western society as it was in first-century Rome.

It is also true that those of us who are Christians declare that there is one God with our lips but with our lives often serve a whole host of lesser loyalties—little gods that we make equal to the God who is God.

In one community where I served as pastor, a community I dearly love, the local newspaper listed church services each week under the headline: "Our Faith in Hyde Park." The phrase was supposed to suggest that we who lived in Hyde Park had faiths that claimed our loyalties on Saturday or Sunday. Yet the line captured a clearer truth. Those of us who lived in that neighborhood did have faith in Hyde Park. Hyde Park was a neighborhood in Chicago that had stayed integrated, stable, and comfortable despite the ravages of urban blight around it. We had faith in the university, which is the dominant institution of the community. We had faith in mildly progressive politics of elected officials. We had faith in the power of reasonable discourse and polite persuasion to change policy, at least in our own neighborhood. We had faith that if we stuck together we could maintain high property values.

It may well be that none of these loyalties was inappropriate or unfaithful in itself. Yet our temptation was to place these lesser loyalties on the same level as our loyalty to God. Our lives were full of many good and worthy things, and the temptation was just to add God to that list.

If those of us in Western society listed our gods, the list might include community, family, and professional or artistic or financial success. Perhaps most visibly and most pervasively the nation can become a god. Patriotism vies with faith as the central orientation of our souls. The issue gets most confusing when politicians, whether out of conviction or hypocrisy, try to persuade us that God's ways are their ways. People lead us astray when they suggest that a loyalty to Christ's cause dictates loyalty to a particular party or platform.

The words of Romans will be a challenge to us. There is one God, lord over communities, politics, nations, families, good causes, and great art. Other goods derive their good from God. Other loyalties are judged in the light of our loyalty to God. More powerfully, other loyalties are judged by the God who is God, the God revealed in Jesus Christ. To that God alone we owe our ultimate loyalty and devotion. For Paul, faith can only be faith in *that* God. To live rightly is to live by faith.

THE GOD OF SCRIPTURE

A word needs to be said about the way in which Paul writes of the one true God. Paul is not primarily a philosopher. He is an apostle and preacher, and, like later preachers, his thinking starts from scripture. For Paul, of course, scripture is the Hebrew Bible—our Old Testament. The sources of his reflection about God are that Bible, on the one hand, and the proclamation of the life, death, and resurrection of Jesus Christ, on the other.

We have already seen in passages we have quoted that Paul often bases his claims concerning God's oneness on his reading of scripture (see Rom. 10:11, 13; 11:34–35).

We shall see later that two verses from scripture provide the starting point for Paul's understanding of the way in which all people can know the blessing of the one true God. Those two verses are Habakkuk 2:4 and Genesis 15:6.

In Romans 1:17 ("The one who is righteous will live by faith"), which concludes the introduction to his letter, Paul is quoting Habakkuk 2:4. That sentence can also be translated, "The one who is righteous through faith will live." We shall see that Paul really makes both of these claims about the significance of faith in the one God. Paul interprets the text in such a way that we can see that he cares about both how to live now and who will have life forever.

In Romans 4:3, in his great discussion of Abraham as the example of faith and the father of all faithful people, Jews and Gentiles alike, Paul quotes Genesis 15:6: "For what does the scripture say? 'Abraham believed God [had faith in God], and it was reckoned to him as righteousness.' "

We see in these passages that two key ideas for Paul come together—God's righteousness and our faith. Paul believes that God wills and does what is right for every person and for the whole creation. The way we lay hold of that rightness is by faith. True faith is faith in the one true God who wills what is right for all creation.

As we study Romans, we shall be studying the ways in which Paul uses the story of Jesus and the words of the Old Testament as the basis for the good news he wants to share with the churches at Rome.

NEW WORLD: NEW AGE

In the United States, at least, we always seem to be looking for a new and better world. Franklin Delano Roosevelt declared that he provided the American people with a New Deal. John Kennedy led us toward a New Frontier, and Bill Clinton tried briefly to declare a New Covenant. Our longing for a new world has deep roots in the Bible and in the hopes of Jews and Christians for a new heaven and a new earth.

In addition to his claim that God is the one God revealed in Jesus Christ and acknowledged through faith, Paul makes another claim throughout Romans. He claims that in Jesus Christ the shift of the ages has come: the new heaven and the new earth are on their way. These two themes play off against each other throughout the epistle in a kind of counterpoint. They are both part of the gospel, the good news Paul declares.

Along with many Jewish people of his time, Paul had waited with eager expectation for the moment when the old age, the age of oppression and sin and distress, would pass away. In the new age God would establish complete rule over all creation. Justice and mercy would flourish. Those who had been faithful to God's will as it was revealed in the Torah, the commandments of the Hebrew Bible, would join in the salvation that God had promised. Perhaps their faithfulness to the Torah, the law, would point to that coming salvation. It may be that Paul, like many other Jews, believed that a messiah, a king anointed by God, would be the one who would bring God's new age on earth as God's appointed servant.

Now to Paul's astonishment the new age has begun, but in the oddest possible way. It has not begun because of people's faithful obedience to the law. It has begun through the execution and resurrection of an outlaw, Jesus, the unlikely Messiah. It is this outlaw who is the fulfillment of the law, the Torah. In the new age, which Jesus the outlaw brings, God is God of all. God is not only God of all who obey the law. God is the God of all who have faith in Jesus.

We see how our themes, the oneness of God and the shift of the ages, come together in Paul's thought.

Throughout our study of Romans we shall see the ways in which Paul writes about this shift of the ages. The shift of the ages has begun in Jesus Christ. It is confirmed by the gift of God's Spirit. It is to be completed when "the creation itself will be set free from its bondage to decay and will obtain the freedom of the glory of the children of God" (Rom. 8:21).

What is clear from the start is that though the shift of the ages is not yet complete, it has begun in Jesus Christ. As believers, the Roman Christians live in two ages—the age of sin, which is passing away, and the age of God's righteousness, which is breaking in. But their loyalty is clearly in the new age, and their lives are lived as citizens of that age.

> How can we who died to sin go on living in it? Do you not know that all of us who have been baptized into Christ Jesus were baptized into his death? Therefore we have been buried with him by baptism into death, so that, just as Christ was raised from the dead by the glory of the Father, so we too might walk in newness of life. (Rom. 6:2–4)

Paul uses the fact that the Roman Christians are citizens of the new age as the grounds for exhorting them to live as faithful persons.

> I appeal to you therefore, brothers and sisters, by the mercies of God, to present your bodies as a living sacrifice, holy and acceptable to God, which is your spiritual worship. Do not be conformed to this world [age], but be

transformed by the renewing of your minds, so that you may discern what is the will of God—what is good and acceptable and perfect. (Rom. 12:1–2)

Paul's understanding of the shift between the old age and the new seems very strange to us. We have some sense of what he means by the claim that there is only one God over all people, and from time to time we acknowledge the truth of that claim. But the claim that we live in a new age, a reign of God, which is breaking in on the old age—that is very hard for us to comprehend, and even harder to believe.

Some of us think that history will simply go on in much the same way it always has for the indefinite future. God may be God, but history is largely the result of human decisions and of impersonal forces like the stock market and the weather. We may pray to God to help us make better decisions, but we don't expect God to do much about history or about the market or about the weather.

Others think that history is a mess and expect God to rescue us from the mess later or, we hope, sooner. We check the signs that the end may be near and wait for a time when God will either take the faithful to heaven or establish Christ's visible reign on earth.

Paul believes that God is in charge of history and that God's new age has already begun. The world that is full of sin and distress is real enough but on its way out; the world that is full of grace and peace is real enough and to spare, full measure and running over. For those with eyes to see what God has done in Jesus Christ and faith to accept God's doing, a new world has already begun. The new age will be completed in a way and in a time we do not begin to understand, but we do not wait for that complete fulfillment to act out our citizenship.

In our time, as in Paul's, we make a fundamental choice about how we see the world. We may see history as a "tale told by an idiot, full of sound and fury, signifying nothing" (*Macbeth*, act 3, scene 5). From that perspective Jesus' death is just one more sign of how bad things can be. Or we can see history in the light of Jesus' death and resurrection. From that perspective, despite the futility and despair we sometimes see and feel, God will have the last word, and that last word is already evident in Jesus Christ. God's word is a word of hope and it points toward the fullness of God's reign.

Paul's claim comes very close to what Jesus says in Mark's Gospel at the very beginning of his own ministry: "The time is fulfilled, and the kingdom of God has come near" (Mark 1:14). Jesus declares that the time of waiting is over. God's kingdom is more than near, it is at hand. The kingdom has one foot in the door.

To put it another way, we could say that for Paul human history is in its adolescence. The old and childish ways are passing away (though occasional temper tantrums and childish selfishness break out). A new maturity of justice and kindness is coming. You can see all the signs. You wait with eager longing for history to finish growing up. Any minute now. We know history is growing up because we know Jesus, the one perfectly obedient, perfectly adult person. He is a sign of what God intends for us all and for all creation.

It is also clear that Paul's idea of the new age breaking in in Jesus Christ is very far from most of what is called the "new age" movement in our own time. For Paul the center of history is not signified by astrological wonders or obscure predictions. For Paul the center of history is the cross of Jesus Christ. When the whole creation comes together, it will come together in praise and devotion to him. A Presbyterian pastor from Ghana suggested that the cross of Christ is like the compass mark on a globe. It reaches north and south, east and west. In Christ the whole world hangs together. That is the new age which Christians believe and serve, the new age Paul proclaims.

By his use of scripture and the story about Jesus, Paul declares his gospel. The old age is passing away. The new age is breaking in. In the new age God establishes God's right to be God over all creation. Blessed are those who receive that news in faith.

That is what Paul wants the Romans to hear—and believe. When he introduces himself, he introduces this good news, too.

1. Salutation and Thanksgiving
Romans 1:1–17

THE SALUTATION
Romans 1:1–7

1:1 **Paul, a servant of Jesus Christ, called to be an apostle, set apart for the gospel of God, 2 which he promised beforehand through his prophets in the holy scriptures, 3 the gospel concerning his Son, who was descended from David according to the flesh 4 and was declared to be Son of God with power according to the spirit [or Spirit] of holiness by resurrection from the dead, Jesus Christ our Lord, 5 through whom we have received grace and apostleship to bring about the obedience of faith among all the Gentiles for the sake of his name, 6 including yourselves who are called to belong to Jesus Christ,**

7 To all God's beloved in Rome, who are called to be saints:
Grace to you and peace from God our Father and the Lord Jesus Christ.

When we write letters today we usually follow a traditional form. The letter begins with "Dear," with the name of the person to whom we are writing, and the letter ends with "Sincerely," or "Cordially" or "Love," followed by our signature.

In Paul's time, letter writers also followed a formula, but it was somewhat different from ours. The letter began with the name of the person who wrote it, then moved quickly to the name of the person receiving the letter. This opening "salutation" closed with a word of greeting. The first paragraph of a letter therefore looked something like this: "Lucius to Lydia. Greetings!"

Of course the salutation could also be expanded to provide useful information, or to set something of the agenda for the letter to follow: "Lucius, cloth merchant, to Lydia, dyer and valued client, and her household. Greetings!"

Paul takes the simple form of the salutation and expands it greatly to make the points he wants to make. The salutation tells us much about Paul himself. It tells a good deal about his understanding of the Roman Christians. It begins to declare the good news, the gospel, that is at the heart of the letter.

At its simplest, Paul's salutation says this: "Paul to the Christians at Rome. Grace to you!" But Paul does not leave the salutation at its simplest.

Who Is Paul?

The salutation begins: "Paul, a servant [or slave] of Jesus Christ, called to be an apostle, set apart for the gospel [or good news] of God" (Rom. 1:1).

In many of his other letters, Paul begins the letter by calling himself an apostle. Here he begins by calling himself Jesus' servant, or slave. Perhaps this is because Paul did not found the church at Rome and is not *their* apostle as he was apostle to the churches at Corinth or at Galatia. He did not found the church at Rome, so he begins with an even broader claim. He is a servant, or slave, of Jesus Christ.

On the one hand, this is a humble claim. Paul's ministry is not from himself or for himself. He stands entirely under the authority of Jesus Christ. His job is to do what Christ tells him to do. On the other hand, this is a bold claim. Throughout Romans Paul draws on scripture (our Old Testament) to help the Romans understand the workings of God. In the Old Testament, "servant of the Lord" is often used as a title for those figures of great authority chosen by God to speak God's word. In Amos 3:7 and Jeremiah 7:25, for instance, the prophets are called God's servants. In Joshua 1:2 Moses is called the servant of the Lord, and the term "servant" is used for Joshua and David elsewhere in the Old Testament.

Certainly Paul sees himself as standing in the tradition of the prophets, as one called by God and speaking God's own word to humankind. For instance when he describes his own call in Galatians 1:15–16, he does so in terms that remind us of Jeremiah's call. Paul says:

> But when God, who had set me apart before I was born and called me through his grace, was pleased to reveal his Son to me [or "in me" or "by me"], so that I might proclaim him among the Gentiles, I did not confer with any human being. (Gal. 1:15–16)

Compare that with Jeremiah's call:

> Now the word of the LORD came to me saying,
>   "Before I formed you in the womb I knew you,
>   and before you were born I consecrated you;
>   I appointed you a prophet to the nations."
>   (Jer. 1:4–5)

Now Paul moves to the title he often uses: "Called to be an apostle." The word "apostle" comes from the verb that means "to send." An apostle is one who is sent by God or by Jesus Christ. As God's messenger, the apostle, like the prophet, carries God's own authority. He is able to speak for God. For Paul this is always a loving authority. Paul's tender affection for the churches is evident in everything he writes, although sometimes he can write very sternly.

For Paul, his authority as an apostle derives from the fact that he has seen the risen Lord and been commissioned to preach the gospel, especially to the Gentiles.

Paul does not stress that he has seen the risen Lord in this passage, but it is central to his understanding of his own apostleship, as we can see in 1 Corinthians 9:1–2 and in 1 Corinthians 15:1–11. Although Paul was not a member of the circle of those who followed Jesus during his ministry in Galilee and Judea, like the other apostles, he did see the risen Christ.

Paul does stress the other side, or aspect, of his apostolic authority. He has been commissioned as a messenger to preach the gospel. He says that he is *called* to be an apostle (see also Gal. 1:11–16; 2 Cor. 5:19–20). As an apostle Paul insists that he is called by God, like the prophets. His apostleship is not something he chose for himself, but something for which God chose him. No apostle, no messenger for God, is an apostle by his or her own choice alone. Apostles are invited, commanded, called to be apostles by the mercy of God.

Paul has another way of talking about his special mission. He is not only called; he is "set apart for the gospel of God." Paul's authority resides not only in the fact that God called him and set him aside, but in the message God gave him, the good news of the gospel.

Because he has been called by God and entrusted with the gospel, Paul has the authority of an apostle. It is precisely his authority that Paul is eager to assert as he begins his letter to the Roman Christians. Most of them do not know him. He did not found their community, nor has he served as its leader, so he needs to persuade them of his authority. To put it simply, he needs to persuade them that they should listen to what he has to say. [1]

There is a bumper sticker that says simply: "Question authority." Authority has had a bad press in our time. We do not like other people telling us what to believe or what to do. We resist any leaders who seem to us to be "authoritarian." Authoritarian leaders are those who would boss us around and ask us to obey, often unquestioningly. Whatever their titles or credentials or positions, they are bullies. They do not ask what we want or need but tell us what they think we should want and need. We resist them because they threaten our freedom and deny our dignity.

There are other leaders, however, who are not so much "authoritarian" as "authoritative." We turn to them for guidance because we trust them to be both truthful and helpful. My physician is such an authoritative figure for me—not perfect, not God—but wise, well trained, and concerned for my well-being. Women and men who have served as my pastors, both officially and unofficially, are people I trust because their lives show their faith in God and their concern for me and for other people.

Paul as an apostle is an authoritative and not an authoritarian figure. His authority isn't that of a bully but that of a loving teacher, pastor, healer. His authority does not come from his love of being in charge. His authority comes from the claim God has laid upon him. He does not just announce his own opinions. He tells the good news of the gospel that is given for the healing of all humankind. Paul writes out of a very deep concern for the Roman Christians. Through the years, the whole church, and not just the Roman community of the first century, has heard Paul's words as addressed to us. We have claimed the book of Romans as scripture and Paul as a true apostle and servant of Jesus Christ.

As Christians we test other authoritative church leaders in part by how well they mirror Paul's love of God, his zeal for the gospel, his passion for God's people.

Who Are the Roman Christians?

Paul refers to the Christians at Rome as those who are "called to belong to Jesus Christ" (Rom. 1:6), who are "called to be saints," and who are "beloved" of God (1:7). Just as Paul is called to be an apostle, the Romans are called to be Christ's people, each of them with his or her own particular gifts. There are distinctions among people and their ministries in Paul, but every Christian is called. To say that Christians are called is to say that Christian identity does not come first from our decision for God. Christian identity comes first from God's decision for us. No Christian is a Christian by his or her choice alone. Paul is not an apostle by his own accomplishment or even by his own decision. God has called him. We are not Christians by our accomplishment or even first by our own decision: God has called us.

The contemporary practice by which only people wishing to be ordained are supposed to talk about their "call" would be foreign to Paul. To him, every Christian has been called; that is what makes the person a Christian. Whether or not Christians can point to a particular moment when we recognize the call, in Jesus Christ God has called us all. That is what makes us Christians. In our time and in our terms we would say that Paul is much more concerned with baptism than with ordination. At baptism every Christian acknowledges that he or she is called into the community of faith. At ordination we acknowledge the gifts of certain Christian leaders, but in fact each of us has special gifts, and all of us share in the fundamental call to be God's people in Jesus Christ.

When Paul says that the Roman Christians are "saints," he means simply that they belong to Jesus Christ. Paul's term for "Christian" is usually "saint." Saints are not some special subgroup of Christians whom the church acknowledges as being unusually pious or prayerful, zealous for good works or doers of miracles. Saints are Christian people—God's family in Jesus Christ. In Greek the word "saint" is a form of the word "holy." Paul insists that life in Jesus Christ is made visible in the holiness, the sanctity, the saintliness of the saints. We shall see that Romans 12—14 describes in great detail what true saintliness looks like. Here we need to remember that for Paul saintliness is the mark of every Christian's life, not the special quality of a few.

When Paul calls the Christians "God's beloved," he sheds light on the gospel he wishes to declare to them. That gospel is that God's love for the whole creation is proclaimed and enacted in Jesus Christ. This little band of Christians at Rome is the group of people who acknowledge, know, and knowingly receive God's love. In that sense they are God's beloved. Here, as in the Gospel of John, we are told that God loves the whole creation, but some people have been called and gifted to acknowledge and share that love (see John 3:16–17).

God's love for the whole creation is part of what Paul means by the good news he wants to share with the Roman "saints."

What Is Paul's Gospel?

Paul says that he has been "set apart for the gospel of God" (Rom. 1:1). The gospel to which Paul refers is not one of our four Gospels—Matthew, Mark, Luke, or John. All of these were written later than Romans and probably after Paul's lifetime. The word "gospel" means "good news," or "good message." As an apostle, as one who is sent, Paul has been entrusted with a good message, the best imaginable.

In his 1525 Prologue to the New Testament, the English translator William Tyndale defined the gospel in ways faithful to Paul's own understanding: "*Euangelio* (that we call gospel) is a Greek word, and signifieth good, merry, glad and joyful tidings, that maketh a man's heart glad, and maketh him sing, dance, and leap for joy."

The gospel message is both old and new. It is old because it begins with the promises of God. Paul writes of "the gospel of God, which he promised beforehand through his prophets in the holy scriptures" (Rom. 1:2). Paul believes that the prophets pointed to Jesus Christ and that faithful people can find in scripture—in the Old Testament—the evidence that from the beginning God planned to work salvation through God's son. Some versions of the Christian faith make it sound as if by about 4 B.C. God's plans had all failed so God had to try something new and decided to send Jesus Christ. Paul believes that Jesus Christ was part of God's plan from the start, and Paul says that if we read the Old Testament with the eyes of faith we can see that that is true.

The gospel message is also new, because it is a message concerning God's son. And now the coming of God's son is not some future event. It has already happened. What the prophets and the Old Testament writers anticipated has now come to pass. The old promise is now fulfilled.

Paul's description of the contents of the gospel uses language that seems a bit different from his usual style:

> . . . the gospel concerning his Son, who was descended from David according to the flesh and was declared to be Son of God with power according to the spirit of holiness by resurrection from the dead, Jesus Christ our Lord . . . (Rom. 1:3–4)

What strikes some people as unusual about this passage is Paul's apparent claim that Jesus was "declared to be Son of God" (only) at his resurrection. Paul usually affirms that Jesus was son of God from the beginning. We can see this both in Romans 8:3 and 8:32, and elsewhere, in Galatians 4:4. So some have thought that Paul might be quoting a saying or a hymn that the Roman Christians would recognize, but which does not say exactly what Paul would say on his own.

Even today, a favorite hymn may have some lines that say exactly what we believe. Some other portion of the hymn may talk about our faith differently from the way we would talk, but we still love the hymn and sing it and quote it whether we agree with every word or not.

However, we have seen that one of Paul's great claims is that the new age of God's mercy is breaking into history in Jesus Christ. Paul talks about the old age as the age "according to the flesh"; he talks about the new age as the age "according to the spirit." If Paul is thinking that way in Romans 1:3–4, then he means something like this:

> I proclaim the gospel of God, the gospel concerning God's son, who according to the standards of the old age, with its concern for the Jewish law and for family connections, was David's son.
> But in the new age, through faith, we can see that Jesus is really God's son, and the fact that Jesus is God's son is made evident in the resurrection.

Furthermore, Paul suggests, by the standards of the old age Jesus might belong only to David's people, the Jews, because Jesus was David's son, and David was king of the Jews. However, in the new age, Jesus belongs to all people—Jews and Gentiles alike—because he is God's son, and God is ruler of everyone.

I prefer the note in the NRSV which says that Jesus was declared Son of God by the Spirit of holiness, not by the spirit of holiness. (The Greek manuscripts on which our translations of the New Testament are based do not make any distinction between capital and lowercase letters.) For Paul the Spirit is God's ongoing gift of power and wisdom to believers. So, whatever the original hymn may have said, surely for Paul it is the Holy Spirit who confirms our faith in Jesus as God's own son. Furthermore, in this context, it may be that it is God's Spirit who confirms Jesus as Son of God in the resurrection. It may be impossible to recover exactly how Paul understands the relationship between the Spirit as the one who instills faith in us and the Spirit as the one who confirms Jesus as God's son.

So Paul writes that through Jesus Christ "we have received grace and apostleship to bring about the obedience of faith among all the Gentiles [or among all the nations, including the Gentiles] for the sake of his name" (Rom. 1:5). The gifts of grace and apostleship that Paul has received through Jesus Christ are also part of the gospel, the good message, that he proclaims. "Grace" is Paul's word for the undeserved goodness we receive absolutely freely from God out of God's great generosity, the goodness we receive in Jesus Christ. Grace means that for Christians every morning is Christmas morning, bright with gifts and wonderful surprises—

bright with the gift of Christ himself. "Apostleship" is Paul's word for his own calling, as one who is sent with the message of grace.

"The obedience of faith," or "faithful obedience," is a phrase Paul uses only here and in Romans 16:26, where again the purpose of the gospel is to bring about "the obedience of faith." Our epistle begins and ends with this great theme. In 10:16 Paul also writes of those who have not all "obeyed the good news." Romans is full of the claim that we accept God's goodness to us through faith. In these three passages, however, we see that faith also carries with it the responsibility of obeying God's gospel. On the one hand, obeying the gospel means heeding the gospel, hearing it, paying attention. Faith is itself obedience. On the other hand, faithful people are obedient in every aspect of their lives: those who hear the gospel bear the fruits of obedience. The faithful are also the "saints." The faithful life is the life of holiness as well. "Faith" and "obedience" are closely linked in Romans. In Romans 15:18 Paul says that his goal has been to "win obedience from the Gentiles," while in 10:14 Paul suggests that the goal of his preaching has been to inspire faith. In 1:8 it is the "faith" of the Roman Christians that is well known. In 16:19 it is their "obedience." Faith and obedience are two sides of the same coin. Real faith is obedient; real obedience is faithful. Faith that is not obedient is just lip service. Obedience that does not include faith is just frenzy.

At the end of the salutation, Paul uses two terms that again help sum up his gospel: "Grace to you and peace" (Rom. 1:7).

"*Grace to you.*" The usual greeting at the beginning of a letter in Paul's day was the word "greeting," which sounded in Greek almost like the word "grace." Paul changes the word slightly and the point greatly. Now it is not just Paul's greeting that his letter carries; it also carries God's grace, God's goodness given freely in Jesus Christ. That goodness is now written up, wrapped up, in a letter, Paul's gift to the faithful people in Rome.

"*Peace to you.*" When Paul writes "peace," he surely thinks of the Hebrew word *shalom*, still a greeting among Jewish people today. *Shalom* means not just the absence of conflict but wholeness, completeness—a trusting relationship toward God and toward one another. As faith is lived out in obedience, grace is made manifest in peace.

Grace and peace are not Paul's to give: "Grace to you and peace from God our Father and the Lord Jesus Christ" (Rom. 1:7). The apostle brings the gifts with which he is sent. The messenger declares the message with which he has been entrusted. Grace. Peace. Good news. Gospel.

In seeking to explain the meaning of the term "gospel," Martin Luther quotes these verses from the opening of Romans and concludes:

There you have it. The gospel is a story about Christ, God's and David's Son, who died and was raised and is established as Lord. This is the gospel in a nutshell. Just as there is no more than one Christ, so there is and may be no more than one gospel. Since Paul and Peter too teach nothing but Christ, in the way we have just described, so their epistles can be nothing but the gospel.

(*A Brief Instruction on What to Look for and Expect in the Gospels*, quoted in Lischer, ed., *Theories of Preaching*, 96)

THE THANKSGIVING
Romans 1:8–17

1:8 **First, I thank my God through Jesus Christ for all of you, because your faith is proclaimed throughout the world. 9 For God, whom I serve with my spirit by announcing the gospel of his Son, is my witness that without ceasing I remember you always in my prayers, 10 asking that by God's will I may somehow at last succeed in coming to you. 11 For I am longing to see you so that I may share with you some spiritual gift to strengthen you— 12 or rather so that we may be mutually encouraged by each other's faith, both yours and mine. 13 I want you to know, brothers and sisters, that I have often intended to come to you (but thus far have been prevented), in order that I may reap some harvest among you as I have among the rest of the Gentiles. 14 I am a debtor both to Greeks and to barbarians, both to the wise and to the foolish 15 —hence my eagerness to proclaim the gospel to you also who are in Rome.**

16 For I am not ashamed of the gospel; it is the power of God for salvation to everyone who has faith, to the Jew first and also to the Greek. 17 For in it the righteousness of God is revealed through faith for faith; as it is written, "The one who is righteous will live by faith."

After the salutation, Paul moves to a section of the letter scholars call the "thanksgiving." New Testament scholar Paul Schubert, in a book called *The Form and Function of Pauline Thanksgivings*, showed that most of Paul's letters begin with a thanksgiving, a paragraph where Paul tells the Christians about his prayers for them. The only exception is Galatians, where we can see that Paul is not grateful for the Galatians at all when he writes this letter. He is just angry at them.

Schubert showed that time after time Paul reveals the main themes of his letters in this opening thanksgiving section. In this, Paul acts a little like contemporary preachers who use the pastoral prayer to preview or summarize the morning's sermon. They are thanking God with one eye on the congregation. Paul thanks God with one eye on the Romans.

One very practical theme is evident in this thanksgiving section of Romans. Paul wants very much to visit Rome. He starts out talking about this wish in a way that may sound a little conceited: "For I am longing to see you so that I may share with you some spiritual gift to strengthen you" (Rom. 1:11). However, Paul quickly revises his wish to show that his relationship to the Romans must be one of mutual care: "For I am longing to see you so that I may share with you some spiritual gift to strengthen you—or rather so that we may be mutually encouraged by each other's faith, both yours and mine."

Paul's revision of his claim toward greater mutuality may represent appropriate reluctance to claim too much authority over a church he did not found. In any case, his revision is a reminder to all people who serve as Christian leaders. In the church all of us, like the apostles, depend on the gifts of other Christians. Christian leadership is always a matter of mutual love, concern, upbuilding.

Paul also expresses his thanks for the faith or faithfulness of the Romans. The Greek word *pistis* can mean either one. "First, I thank my God through Jesus Christ for all of you, because your faith [or faithfulness] is proclaimed throughout the world" (Rom. 1:8). This suggests that the spiritual gift with which Paul is most concerned is the gift of faith. The whole letter to the Romans can be seen as the means by which Paul seeks to "share the spiritual gift" of faith in order to strengthen the Romans. Since he cannot be there in person to provide that gift, the letter becomes the gift.

We can also see that Paul is aware that many of the members of the churches at Rome are Gentiles, since he says he hopes to "reap some harvest among you as I have among the rest of the Gentiles" (Rom. 1:13).

Romans 1:16-17 marks the end of Paul's thanksgiving and the beginning of the main business of the letter. In these verses Paul begins to share the spiritual gift of faith with the Romans.

When Paul says he is not ashamed of this good news, that is probably not because someone has suggested that he ought to be ashamed or that there is something shameful about the gospel. It is more likely an indirect way of saying: I take great pride in this good news, not in myself, but in the news I proclaim. I have great confidence in this gospel.

Yet for us the phrase may take on a slightly different meaning. We are glad enough to be Christians but often not glad to talk much about our faith. It may even be embarrassing to admit that we take time each week for worship. Political leaders ask for our prayers and pronounce God's blessing on us, but as Christian individuals we have a hard time admitting that we turn to prayer and depend absolutely on God's blessing. Teaching in a secular university, I sometimes find it easier not to confess that I teach at the "divinity" school. When arguing about social issues outside of church or seminary, I am sometimes hesitant to confess that my opinions are based partly on Christian convictions: on Bible study and prayer. Many of us love the gospel in our hearts but are afraid to admit our love out loud.

Now we learn a remarkable fact about this gospel, this good message, this good news. It is power. It does things; it makes a difference. Genuine good news always makes a difference. "We're going to have a baby!" "You got the job!" "The surgery was successful!" News is different from gossip or information. It changes the way we live. Good news changes the way we live for the better.

Paul says that his good news, the good news about Jesus Christ, not only makes our lives better, it brings salvation. We should not assume we know what Paul means by "salvation." We tend to think that the question "Are you saved?" means "Are you going to heaven when you die?" Paul certainly believes that death will not separate believers from the love of God. We shall see, however, that for Paul salvation is a promise for the future that has implications for the present. Salvation is a promise to the whole creation and not just to individual believers.

Because the gospel brings salvation, it has power. Remember that in Romans 1:4 we learned that Jesus was declared Son of God with power. Now that same power that made Christ Son of God empowers believers for salvation—through the gospel.

Yet it is believers, those who have faith, who acknowledge God's power in the good news. It is not just Jewish believers and not just Gentile believers who will receive salvation. The gospel is power "to the Jew first and also to the Greek." This again is Paul's way of saying that the one God is the God of all people, and the way we acknowledge God as God is through faith in Jesus Christ. Paul will also show in Romans 9—11 that in human history salvation has come first to Jews and then to Gentiles.

Now Paul tells us why the gospel has the power to save: "For in it the righteousness of God is revealed through faith for faith" (Rom. 1:17).

"The righteousness of God" is a central theme for Paul, a phrase he loves to use. It is impossible to define what Paul means by God's righteousness in a phrase or two. In some ways the whole book of Romans is a presentation of God's righteousness. However, I can make some initial suggestions now and expand on them as we continue our study of this letter.

First, the righteousness of God is the righteousness of God's own self.

God is righteous. God does right. God is upright. God has perfect integrity. What God promises, God does.

Second, the righteousness of God is the justice God shows in dealing with humankind. God condemns sin. God acts against all oppression and inhumanity. God works and wills to bring all persons into a loving relationship with God and with one another, indeed to bring all creation into community.

Third, the righteousness of God is a gift God gives to faithful people. Paul says that God makes righteous those who have faith. That is, God gives God's own rightness to those who trust in the just, righteous, and loving God. We have a right relationship with God when we accept God's righteousness.

We have seen human communities that provide dim mirrors to the righteousness Paul writes about. We have seen families where the parents or parent seek to live lives of integrity, honesty, justice. In such families each member is treated openly, lovingly. In such families the hope is that children will also grow in justice, uprightness, the capacity to love. We have seen friendships where each member grows in openness and caring because of the mutuality of the relationship. We have seen congregations that nurture members toward trust in God and one another. We have seen political movements that push society toward justice.

Of course, the best human communities and movements fall short of the righteousness of God, but such human communities may help us see how God's righteousness can be manifested in different ways, and yet be one righteousness, one way of being God. God is whole in God's self and whole in God's relationships. To have faith in that God is to know something of God's wholeness for ourselves.

It is also evident for Paul that God's righteousness is active righteousness. God does what is just. God brings about right, loving relationships. The place—the person—in whom God does this is Jesus Christ. For Paul, Jesus Christ is the righteousness of God.

Though Paul may not have known some of the Gospel stories we know, we can read the Gospels and see in the stories of Jesus the righteousness of God. We see in Jesus perfect integrity. He does what he commands. He commands forgiveness and is forgiving. He calls for courage and is courageous. We see in Jesus justice and kindness toward humankind. We see him drive the money changers from the temple and welcome sinners to his table. We see Jesus give the gift of rightness to others: sinners forgiven, isolated people brought into community, ordinary people called to discipleship. Above all, we see the cross where God's judgment against human pettiness and disobedience hangs high on a hill for all to see. We see the cross where God's mercy to all—even to Christ's persecutors—stretches out open arms, embracing humankind. Jesus Christ lives out the righteousness of God.

We have seen that Paul believes that the church lives at the intersection between the old age and the new age. God's righteousness will only be completely established at the final victory of God's glory. Yet that righteousness already has power and force in history and especially among the faithful. That righteousness is revealed in Jesus Christ and will be accomplished when God completes the vindication God began in Christ's resurrection.

When Paul says that in the gospel the righteousness of God is revealed "through faith for faith" (more literally, "from faith to faith") he makes it clear that faith is not a matter of believing the right things or even of doing the right things. Faith is a matter of receiving the gift of God's righteousness in Jesus Christ. Faith is a matter of trusting in the righteousness of God. To those who have such faith, Paul's good news is good news indeed—full of power. Paul may also be saying, as theologian Karl Barth has suggested, that God's righteousness is revealed from God's faithfulness to our faith. God is always faithful to us; when we accept God's faithfulness, we are made right, too (Barth, *Romans*, 42).

Paul closes this thanksgiving section with a quotation from the prophet Habakkuk (Hab. 2:4). The quotation can be translated in two ways. "The one who is righteous will live by faith" (as the NSRV translates it), or "The one who is righteous through faith will live" (as in the NRSV note).

The letter to the Romans suggests that Paul means both these claims when he quotes Habakkuk. The one who has a right relationship to the righteous God has that relationship through faith. He or she lives by faith: walks, eats, breathes, argues, hopes, loves—through faith. Those who have a right relationship with God live in faithful obedience. They trust God to be with them, to strengthen them, to use them for the sake of God's own goodness and justice.

But in addition the one who has this right relationship to the righteous God through faith will have real life, both in this world and in the world to come, both now and eternally. Real life *is* life lived trustingly and obediently with God. And life lived with God cannot end with death, because it is life with *God*. God is stronger than death.

Now we return to the themes with which we began our study of Romans. How shall we live, in our time, when people believe in no god or in many gods? Paul says we can live only through faith in the one God who is God.

Through faith in the one God who is God we are spared the terrible anxiety of playing off one loyalty against another: our love of country against our love of family against our love of success. Faith, total trust in the God who is God, shifts all that. Instead of dashing from loyalty to loyalty, altar to altar, commitment to commitment, we give our loyalty to God, and all lesser loyalties find their meaning in that basic trust.

The awful word "prioritize" has crept into our language. It points to a legitimate need. In the midst of competing claims on our time and attention, how do we decide the order of their importance? The letter to the Romans would suggest that because God is "prior," before all loyalties, creator of all lesser gods, God always has highest priority. Because God was first, in the beginning, God has first claim on our allegiance. In Jesus Christ, God makes that claim—once, for all.

Through faith in the one God who is God of all we are spared the false certainty that our way is the only way. We no longer assume that God has validated only our denomination or our theology or our lifestyle. We shun any competitive evangelism or church growth movements that pit one community of faith against another. We deny that God can be captured by any theological movement or any doctrine of scriptural inspiration. We are spared from defending *our* way against every argument, every question, every alternative. Trusting God to be God of all people, we rejoice that God has also chosen us to be God's own. With nothing to defend, we receive God's love with gratitude.

Through faith in the one God we are spared the depressing possibility that we might be it, the final creator of our own goods and goals, the only god we've got. We are no longer required to get up each morning and fashion our own identity. We are no longer required to invent meaning for our lives. We receive the identity we are given in Jesus Christ, and we rejoice in the meaning God has provided in him.

Through faith we place our trust in the righteous God, knowing that, in Jesus Christ, God also makes us right, for now and for eternity.

2. God's Wrath and God's Righteousness
Romans 1:18–4:25

In Romans 1:18–4:25 Paul describes for the Roman Christians that gospel of which he is not ashamed. The clue to the overall claim of this section of the letter is found in a contrast Paul makes. On the one hand, he says, God's wrath is being revealed to all of humankind. On the other hand, God's righteousness is being revealed to all of humankind. This contrast between God's wrath and God's righteousness sets the theme of Romans 1—4.

In Romans 1:18 Paul writes:

> For the wrath of God is revealed from heaven against all ungodliness and wickedness of those who by their wickedness suppress the truth.

(The NRSV translation does not quite catch the power of the present tense: "The wrath of God is—right now—being revealed.") Then, in Romans 3:21–22 Paul makes the contrasting claim:

> But now, apart from law, the righteousness of God has been disclosed, and is attested by the law and the prophets, the righteousness of God through faith in Jesus Christ for all who believe.

(I would prefer: "for all who have faith." The same Greek root word for "faith" or "having faith" is used twice, once as a noun, once as a verb.)

Notice the repetition of "all" in these two claims. God's wrath is being revealed against all who sin (which we shall see means everyone). God's righteousness has been revealed for all who have faith (which we shall see could include everyone). The one God pronounces one judgment on all, but provides one way to escape that judgment: through faith in the one person Jesus Christ.

Also notice the way in which Paul talks about *when* God's wrath and God's righteousness are revealed. God's wrath is being revealed right now; judgment is taking place all around us. But God's righteousness has already been disclosed in a past event, in Jesus Christ, and that righteousness is still powerful and effective among all who have faith. Paul has spoken of the power of the gospel (1:16). That power is so strong that it can overcome not only our sin but God's own wrath. This is not because God has a kind of split personality. It is because the God who wills the right brings the right about both by judging us and by providing us mercy. The one God has one intention for creation, but that intention is evident both in judgment and in loving-kindness.

Think of a parent or relative or teacher who helped shape your life for the good. Weren't judgment and kindness combined in that person? Judgment and discipline served kindness. Kindness tempered discipline. The one who loved you was pushing you and inviting you toward maturity, fullness, uprightness. Just so the righteous God both judges our unrighteousness and mercifully brings us into maturity, fullness, and a right relationship with God's own self.

There is an unanswerable puzzle about Paul's claim. Did Paul begin by noticing the power of sin and the devastation of God's wrath and then rejoice to discover the mercy promised to all in Jesus Christ? Or did Paul discover God's great love in Jesus Christ, and in the light of that goodness discover how badly all people need what God provides? In Jesus Christ what did Paul learn first—God's judgment or God's mercy? My own guess is that Paul understands our need in the light of God's promise, our lack in the light of the gift. The order in which he writes is not the order in which he thinks.

In the book of Acts, Luke tells us the story of Paul's turning from persecuting Christians to becoming a leader of the church. There Paul's own story starts with grace and moves from that to a sense of the depth of sin. It is a self-confident Paul who sets out on the road to Damascus, one sure of himself, not burdened by the knowledge of his secret sins (see Acts 9:1–19). In Philippians, where Paul writes about his own coming to faith, it sounds as though the good news of God in Jesus Christ convinced him that his old goodness was in vain. This would be quite different from the apostle who in Romans describes his former overwhelming sense of sin, overcome by the forgiveness for which he longed.

If anyone else has reason to be confident in the flesh, I have more: circumcised on the eighth day, a member of the people of Israel, of the tribe of Benjamin, a Hebrew born of Hebrews; as to the law, a Pharisee; as to zeal, a persecutor of the church; as to righteousness under the law, blameless.

Yet whatever gains I had, these I have come to regard as loss because of Christ. More than that, I regard everything as loss because of the surpassing value of knowing Christ Jesus my Lord. For his sake I have suffered the loss of all things, and I regard them as rubbish, in order that I may gain Christ and be found in him, not having a righteousness of my own that comes from the law, but one that comes through faith in Christ, the righteousness from God based on faith. (Phil. 3:4b–9)

Whether Paul starts with God's judgment or God's righteousness, for him, to understand God's judgment is to be drawn toward God's righteousness, and to accept God's righteousness is to acknowledge God's judgment.

GOD'S WRATH UPON ALL
Romans 1:18–3:8

Throughout Romans Paul's claim that God is God of all people is especially the claim that God is God both of Jews and of Gentiles. Before Paul can move to the claim that God makes all righteous through Jesus Christ, Paul needs to show that "all have sinned and fall short of the glory of God" (Rom. 3:23). Concretely, he needs to show that Gentiles have sinned and fall short of the glory of God and then that Jews have sinned and fall short of the glory of God.

God's Wrath upon the Gentiles (Romans 1:18–32)

1:18 **For the wrath of God is revealed from heaven against all ungodliness and wickedness of those who by their wickedness suppress the truth.** [19] **For what can be known about God is plain to them, because God has shown it to them.** [20] **Ever since the creation of the world his eternal power and divine nature, invisible though they are, have been understood and seen through the things he has made. So they are without excuse;** [21] **for though they knew God, they did not honor him as God or give thanks to him, but they became futile in their thinking, and their senseless minds were darkened.** [22] **Claiming to be wise, they became fools;** [23] **and they exchanged the glory of the immortal God for images resembling a mortal human being or birds or four-footed animals or reptiles.**
[24] **Therefore God gave them up in the lusts of their hearts to impurity, to the degrading of their bodies among themselves,** [25] **because they exchanged the truth about God for a lie and worshiped and served the creature rather than the Creator, who is blessed forever! Amen.**

26 **For this reason God gave them up to degrading passions. Their women exchanged natural intercourse for unnatural,** 27 **and in the same way also the men, giving up natural intercourse with women, were consumed with passion for one another. Men committed shameless acts with men and received in their own persons the due penalty for their error.**

28 **And since they did not see fit to acknowledge God, God gave them up to a debased mind and to things that should not be done.** 29 **They were filled with every kind of wickedness, evil, covetousness, malice. Full of envy, murder, strife, deceit, craftiness, they are gossips,** 30 **slanderers, God-haters, insolent, haughty, boastful, inventors of evil, rebellious toward parents,** 31 **foolish, faithless, heartless, ruthless.** 32 **They know God's decree, that those who practice such things deserve to die—yet they not only do them but even applaud others who practice them.**

Paul wants to insist that all people have sinned and therefore all people are in need of God's righteousness. For Jews it is clear that sin is breaking of the law, the Torah given by God to Moses. When it comes to the Gentiles, however, there is a problem in talking about sin. Since Gentiles never received the law, how can they be sinners? They cannot be blamed for breaking commandments that were not given them in the first place.

Paul's solution to this problem is to argue that though the Gentiles did not have the stone tablets of the law, they do have the law written on their hearts. This law is evident through the world that God has made, and it can be summed up by the beginning of Moses' own commandments: The Lord God is one. That is, there is a Creator who has made heaven and earth. That Creator is not to be confused with any created thing but stands above all creation. That Creator is one and one only. If there were more than one Creator, there would not be God, only little gods. Paul says that anyone who has eyes to see can see that the world is the work of a Creator but that the world is not itself that Creator. The world belongs to God but cannot be God.

Now, argues Paul, if you know *that*, you know the most important claim of the law, whether or not you ever heard of Moses. And if you know the most important claim of the law, that there is one God, the Creator, then you know that it is God alone who is worthy of our worship and thanks. The Gentiles' sin is this: "though they knew God, they did not honor him as God or give thanks to him."

What they did instead was to give worship and thanks to the things God had made. They worshiped figures of human beings or of animals. Therefore they broke another commandment: the commandment against idolatry. This commandment, too, should have been evident from the world

God has made. So those who broke this commandment are "without excuse" (Rom. 1:20).

The sin that the Gentiles have committed is the sin of idolatry. Then Paul goes on to talk about the consequences of that sin.

> Therefore God gave them up in the lusts of their hearts to impurity. . . . (Rom. 1:24)

> For this reason God gave them up to degrading passions. (1:26)

> And since they did not see fit to acknowledge God, God gave them up to a debased mind and to things that should not be done. (1:28)

We can oversimplify. For Paul the fundamental sin is idolatry: false worship is the way in which Gentiles have fallen short of the glory of God. The punishment, the consequence of that idolatry, takes various forms. Most generally, the punishment consists of impurity and degrading one's body. Neither of these is more specifically defined (Rom. 1:24–25). One example of this impurity consists of certain sexual behavior between people of the same sex (1:26–27).

Another way to talk about the punishment the Gentiles received is to say that God gave them over to "a debased mind" (1:28). Just as the degraded body engages in certain sexual behaviors, the debased mind engages in certain social behaviors: deceit, craftiness, gossip, ruthlessness, and more.

We can put it another way. The lists of behavior and attitude that we often *call* "sins" are for Paul the *consequence* of sin. Sin is the refusal to acknowledge God as God and the eagerness to worship goods that are less than God, created things. For the Gentiles the wages of sin, the consequence of sin, consists of what Paul considers unacceptable sexual behavior and a variety of unacceptable attitudes.

We have seen that Paul is concerned with right relations, with righteousness. For Paul the right relationship to God is to worship God. The right sexual relationship includes heterosexual intercourse. The right interpersonal relationships include consideration, kindness, what he elsewhere calls love (see 1 Corinthians 13). Such relationships do not include envy, deceit, or ruthlessness.

Furthermore, for Paul, the punishment fits the crime. The result of an "unnatural" relationship to God is a series of "unnatural" relationships to other humans. When people exchange the truth about God for a lie (that God is not one and is not creator), they may also exchange "natural" intercourse for "unnatural," that is, heterosexual intercourse for some kind of homosexual intercourse. And they exchange their right mind for a "debased" mind that puffs itself up at the expense of others and of human community.

In recent years Paul's descriptions of sexual behavior among the Gentiles of his time have been used as the basis for heated discussions among Christians about the place of homosexual people and of same-sex relationships within the church.

The issue is a complicated one, and Romans 1 may not shed as much light on the problem as we would think. First, Paul is primarily concerned with issues of idolatry here, and only secondarily with the results of that idolatry in a variety of human behaviors. Second, it is a *variety* of human behaviors that Paul here condemns. Churches that adopt resolutions to exclude homosexual people from their midst do not so quickly read the rest of Romans and also pass resolutions condemning gossip or deceit—practices that in my experience have done considerable damage to the body of Christ. Third, it is not altogether evident just what kinds of behavior Paul here condemns. In *The New Testament and Homosexuality* Robin Scroggs suggests that we may have misunderstood Paul on this issue for centuries. No doubt Paul knew exactly what he was writing about. We do not. Fourth, Paul seems to have little sense that homosexuality may be more a deep-seated orientation than a set of individual choices. We know some things about homosexuality that Paul did not know. He reads his time in the light of the best wisdom available. We are called to read our time in the light of the best wisdom available to us. Fifth, the reason Paul talks about this entire list of consequences of sin is to insist that no one, Jew or Gentile, is free from sin and its consequences and to remind us that all of us receive righteousness from God, not from our own uprightness—or heterosexuality, either. Romans 1 should not be read apart from the whole context of the epistle to the Romans, nor apart from the larger context of Paul's epistles, nor apart from the larger counsel of the New Testament.

Paul's fundamental claim is not a claim about sexual behavior. It is a claim about right worship. Right worship is the worship of the one true God. Gentiles have strayed from that right worship and therefore, by their idolatry, they have fallen "short of the glory of God" (Rom. 3:23).

God's Wrath upon the Jews (Romans 2:1–3:8)

Judging Others (Romans 2:1–16)

2:1 **Therefore you have no excuse, whoever you are, when you judge others; for in passing judgment on another you condemn yourself, because you, the judge, are doing the very same things.** 2 **You say, "We know that God's** judgment on those who do such things is in accordance with the truth." ³ Do you imagine, whoever you are, that when you judge those who do such things and yet do them yourself, you will escape the judgment of God? ⁴ Or do you despise the riches of his kindness and forbearance and patience? Do you not realize that God's kindness is meant to lead you to repentance? ⁵ But by your hard and impenitent heart you are storing up wrath for yourself in the day of wrath, when God's righteous judgment will be revealed. ⁶ For he will repay according to each one's deeds: ⁷ to those who by patiently doing good seek for glory and honor and immortality, he will give eternal life; ⁸ while for those who are self-seeking and who obey not the truth but wickedness, there will be wrath and fury. ⁹ There will be anguish and distress for everyone who does evil, the Jew first and also the Greek, ¹⁰ but glory and honor and peace for everyone who does good, the Jew first and also the Greek. ¹¹ For God shows no partiality.

¹²All who have sinned apart from the law will also perish apart from the law, and all who have sinned under the law will be judged by the law. ¹³ For it is not the hearers of the law who are righteous in God's sight, but the doers of the law who will be justified. ¹⁴ When Gentiles, who do not possess the law, do instinctively what the law requires, these, though not having the law, are a law to themselves. ¹⁵ They show that what the law requires is written on their hearts, to which their own conscience also bears witness; and their conflicting thoughts will accuse or perhaps excuse them ¹⁶ on the day when, according to my gospel, God, through Jesus Christ, will judge the secret thoughts of all.

Though Paul does not begin explicitly by saying that this portion of his argument is addressed to Jews, the chapter that follows makes clear that Jews are the primary audience of this address. (Remember that Paul here addresses the Jews in the Roman congregations as a Jew himself.) "But if you call yourself a Jew and rely on the law . . . " writes Paul in Romans 2:17. And in Romans 2:14, when Paul talks about the Gentiles, it seems clear that they are the people being described, not the people being addressed at the moment.

These verses make clear that the "wrath of God" Paul spoke about at the beginning of this great discussion of sin and justification is not so much God's emotion as God's act. God's wrath is that great judgment by which God will determine the righteousness, uprightness, and right relationship of all humankind. It is the "day of wrath" (2:5). We have seen in reading Romans 1:18 that Paul believes that that day of wrath is already being made manifest: the last days have begun, and the transgressions of the Gentiles are one sign of that judgment.

Now the question, however, is not how the Gentiles, without the law, fall into sin. The question is, How do Jews, who have the law, nonetheless sin? In what ways do they fall short of the glory of God?

The answer is that the Jews fall short of the glory of God first by judging others. Such judgment is mistaken in two ways. It is mistaken because when Jews judge Gentiles in that way they behave in ways that God has already condemned in Gentile behavior. Such judgment is itself "insolent, haughty, boastful" (see Rom. 1:30). Further, such judgment is mistaken because it ignores the fact that the judge is just as sinful as the judged. Jews who have the law break it just as easily as Gentiles who have the law written on their hearts, and they compound the crime by pretending to be innocent. This does not necessarily mean that the Jewish critics violate the law in exactly the same way as the Gentiles, but that they, too, are disobedient to the law they know.

Paul's description of the activity of his fellow Jews (and, one would think, of himself apart from God's righteousness) reminds us of Jesus' parable of the Pharisee and the tax collector. The tax collector, who would be treated like a Gentile by pious Jews, does sin, but at least he knows his sinfulness. The Pharisee sounds like Paul's imaginary Jew, judging the sins of others: "God, I thank you that I am not like other people: thieves, rogues, adulterers, or even like this tax collector" (Luke 18:11).

In Romans 2:12–14 we have a kind of aside where Paul links the first part of the chapter with this second part and points us ahead to the painful, central judgment: "For there is no distinction, since all have sinned and fall short of the glory of God" (3:22–23). In these verses Paul elaborates on that. Gentiles have sinned against the internal law, the law written on their hearts, the law that says that God is one and that we are to worship no false gods or idols. Jews have sinned "under the law," that is, knowing full well what God commanded through Moses, but disobeying those commandments all the same.

Again a word of Jesus is pertinent to Paul's claim here. "Do not judge, so that you may not be judged" (Matt. 7:1). In our churches, denominations, families, and other relationships the temptation is to see what's wrong with everyone else and ignore what's wrong with us. Jesus' exaggeration isn't so exaggerated: "Why do you see the speck in your neighbor's eye, but do not notice the log in your own eye?" (Matt. 7:3). Here we are today, seeing ever so dimly around the two-by-four in our own eye, but sure that we're perceptive enough to spot every mote in the neighbor's eye. Those self-righteous fundamentalists; those sell-out liberals; those self-serving clergy; those pushy laypeople; you pervert; you prig. How often relationships fall apart because confession gives way to accusation, and we point fingers when we should spread our arms to embrace one another.

Perhaps Paul is already looking ahead to his reminders to the Roman Christians in chapter 15. Are Gentiles boasting of their freedom and Jews of their faithfulness? Does this keep them from welcoming one another?

Sin despite the Law (Romans 2:17–3:8)

2:17 But if you call yourself a Jew and rely on the law and boast of your relation to God [18] and know his will and determine what is best because you are instructed in the law, [19] and if you are sure that you are a guide to the blind, a light to those who are in darkness, [20] a corrector of the foolish, a teacher of children, having in the law the embodiment of knowledge and truth, [21] you, then, that teach others, will you not teach yourself? While you preach against stealing, do you steal? [22] You that forbid adultery, do you commit adultery? You that abhor idols, do you rob temples? [23] You that boast in the law, do you dishonor God by breaking the law? [24] For, as it is written, "The name of God is blasphemed among the Gentiles because of you."

[25] Circumcision indeed is of value if you obey the law; but if you break the law, your circumcision has become uncircumcision. [26] So, if those who are uncircumcised keep the requirements of the law, will not their uncircumcision be regarded as circumcision? [27] Then those who are physically uncircumcised but keep the law will condemn you that have the written code and circumcision but break the law. [28] For a person is not a Jew who is one outwardly, nor is true circumcision something external and physical. [29] Rather, a person is a Jew who is one inwardly, and real circumcision is a matter of the heart—it is spiritual and not literal. Such a person receives praise not from others but from God.

3:1 Then what advantage has the Jew? Or what is the value of circumcision? [2] Much, in every way. For in the first place the Jews were entrusted with the oracles of God. [3] What if some were unfaithful? Will their faithlessness nullify the faithfulness of God? [4] By no means! Although everyone is a liar, let God be proved true, as it is written,

"So that you may be justified in your words,
    and prevail in your judging."

[5] But if our injustice serves to confirm the justice of God, what should we say? That God is unjust to inflict wrath on us? (I speak in a human way.) [6] By no means! For then how could God judge the world? [7] But if through my falsehood God's truthfulness abounds to his glory, why am I still being condemned as a sinner? [8] And why not say (as some people slander us by saying that we say), "Let us do evil so that good may come"? Their condemnation is deserved!

Romans 2:17–24 repeats the themes of 2:1–11 and lists the ways in which Jews may boast of their wisdom as those who inherit the law and yet break the very law they claim with pride. The final quotation in verse 24 is based largely on Isaiah 52:5. It sets up a kind of judgment often used by religious communities to enforce ethical rigor. "Look how badly we're doing. Even outsiders laugh at us, and thereby we are causing them to blaspheme God." And in our time there is always the danger that nonbelievers will fail to take God seriously because we believers proclaim one thing with our lips and do something entirely different with our bodies, our votes, our investments.

Romans 2:25–29 is a radical claim that seeks in its own way to break down the ancient distinction between Jews and Gentiles. Here Paul is not talking about the way in which both Gentiles and Jews have broken the law but talking about the ways in which both Gentiles and Jews might live out obedience. For Paul circumcision is a sign of obedience, not a substitute for obedience, and one who obeys without circumcision is still "really," "spiritually," circumcised. Surely here Paul is echoing his concern that the gospel bring about the obedience of faith. But the stress is still on obedience. The reminder that such obedience grows out of faith, *is* faith, will come only in Romans 3. Here Paul is still leading up to his great claim: "There is no distinction."

Romans 3:1–8 looks ahead to themes that will be explained in much greater detail later in the epistle, but here, Paul gives a kind of preview to the Jewish Christians in Rome. He wants to approach two topics that he will soon discuss.

First, the claim that God's righteousness is now given apart from the law does not mean that the law was given for no good reason, or that God's promises to the Jews are overthrown. Far from it. Paul will elaborate on this claim especially in Romans 9—11. Second (and here Paul seems to be looking over his shoulder at those who have misunderstood his gospel), the fact that God overcomes our evil does not mean that we should do all the more evil so that God can be all the more good. Paul will elaborate on this claim especially in Romans 6.

The main theme, however, remains this: Just as the Gentiles have sinned against the law written in their hearts, the Jews have sinned against the law that God gave to Moses. No one has reason to be proud.

THE OLD TESTAMENT
AND GOD'S RIGHTEOUSNESS
Romans 3:9–20

3:9 **What then? Are we any better off? No, not at all; for we have already charged that all, both Jews and Greeks, are under the power of sin,** [10] **as it is written:**

> "There is no one who is righteous, not even one;
> 11   there is no one who has understanding,
>   there is no one who seeks God.
> 12 All have turned aside, together they have become worthless;
>   there is no one who shows kindness,
>   there is not even one."
> 13 "Their throats are opened graves;
>   they use their tongues to deceive."
>   "The venom of vipers is under their lips."
> 14   "Their mouths are full of cursing and bitterness."
> 15 "Their feet are swift to shed blood;
> 16   ruin and misery are in their paths,
> 17 and the way of peace they have not known."
> 18   "There is no fear of God before their eyes."
> 19 Now we know that whatever the law says, it speaks to those who are under the law, so that every mouth may be silenced, and the whole world may be held accountable to God. 20 For "no human being will be justified in his sight" by deeds prescribed by the law, for through the law comes the knowledge of sin.

By quoting these extensive passages from scripture Paul does what he had promised in the beginning of his letter: he shows how the gospel was proclaimed beforehand in the holy scriptures (Rom. 1:2). More than that, because Paul here especially addresses his letter to Jewish Christians, he draws upon the Old Testament to explain the Old Testament. The scripture to which Jews appeal for their self-understanding *itself* tells them that no one is righteous under the law. All have sinned and fallen short of the glory of God. Paul is not saying anything that the scripture has not already said. His word about the law providing knowledge of sin again points ahead to an argument he will make at length in Romans 7. With that aside, he is now ready to move to the ringing confirmation of the argument he has been making: the need of all, Jews and Gentiles alike, for the one righteousness that comes from the one God through the one person Jesus Christ, the righteousness of faith.

THE RIGHTEOUSNESS OF GOD
FOR ALL WHO HAVE FAITH
Romans 3:21–31

> 3:21 But now, apart from law, the righteousness of God has been disclosed, and is attested by the law and the prophets, 22 the righteousness of God through faith in Jesus Christ for all who believe [or "have faith"]. For there

is no distinction, [23] since all have sinned and fall short of the glory of God; [24] they are now justified by his grace as a gift, through the redemption that is in Christ Jesus, [25] whom God put forward as a sacrifice of atonement by his blood, effective through faith. He did this to show his righteousness, because in his divine forbearance he had passed over the sins previously committed; [26] it was to prove at the present time that he himself is righteous and that he justifies the one who has faith in Jesus.

[27] Then what becomes of boasting? It is excluded. By what law? By that of works? No, but by the law of faith. [28] For we hold that a person is justified by faith apart from works prescribed by the law. [29] Or is God the God of Jews only? Is he not the God of Gentiles also? Yes, of Gentiles also, [30] since God is one; and he will justify the circumcised on the ground of faith and the uncircumcised through that same faith. [31] Do we then overthrow the law by this faith? By no means! On the contrary, we uphold the law.

When I attended church camp in my youth, one evening ritual required each camper in our cabin to quote his favorite Bible verse. Each summer some eager Christian would quote Romans 3:23: "For all have sinned and fall short of the glory of God." Of course Paul insists on the fact that all have sinned. But he makes that point in driving toward his main point: All are now justified by God's grace as a gift. That is the good news, the gospel. That is why we have faith, church, and church camps, too.

In order to get some sense of this central affirmation of Paul's we need to remember that the English translation misses the fact that the Greek words for "righteousness" and "just" or "justify" have the same root. The older English phrase "rightwise," meaning "to justify" or "to make right," helps make clear the movement of Paul's argument.

But now apart from law, the *righteousness* of God has been disclosed . . . , the *righteousness* of God through faith in Jesus Christ. . . .

For there is no distinction, since all have sinned and fall short of the glory of God, they are now *rightwised* by his grace as a gift. . . .

(He put forward Christ as a sacrifice of atonement) to show his *righteousness*. . . .

It was to prove at the present time that he himself is *righteous* and that he *rightwises* the one who has faith in Jesus.

Remember that God's righteousness is both God's own justice and goodness and the way in which God brings people into a right relationship with God's own self. And that is the heart of the gospel for Paul: It is *God* who can establish the right relationship. Left to ourselves, we who are Gentiles fall into idolatry and immorality. Left to ourselves, we who are

Jews condemn the Gentiles for their faults as if we are not equally guilty. We are not left to ourselves: In Jesus Christ, God does what is right, makes us right again.

It is also possible, as the note in the margins of the NRSV suggests, that Paul says in 3:26 that God himself "is righteous and that he justifies [right-wises] the one who has the faith of Jesus." If this interpretation is correct, Jesus is a great example of faith. My own reading of the whole book of Romans, influenced by years of reading others' interpretations, still inclines toward the traditional view that it is our faith in Jesus, not Jesus' own faith, that is in view here. Even if it is Jesus' faith, however, the point remains the same. By living out his faith in God in our own lives we accept that righteousness which God does through him and his obedience. (The best argument for the interpretation in the margin of the NRSV is found in Richard Hays, *The Faith of Jesus Christ*, 170–74.)

Faith is our response to God's making us right in Jesus Christ. Faith is not achieving; faith is receiving. Faith is Christmas morning, accepting the gift under the tree, or more important, adoring the child in the manger. Faith stands at Calvary and says: "Surely this was the Son of God." Faith rises on Easter morning to hail the risen Lord. Faith is gratitude and joy—and of course obedience—but the obedience begins with joy.

God's intention is to bring all people into a right relationship with God's self. All people need that right relationship, because all have sinned and fallen short of God's glory. That is to say, all of us have failed to worship God as the one true God. All of us have committed idolatry. Remember that in Romans 1:23 Paul says that the sin of the Gentiles (or perhaps of all humankind) is that "they exchanged the glory of the immortal God for images." Because we fall short of God's glory, only the God of glory can make us right. God does this as a gift. The word for God's gift to us is "grace." Grace *means* gift, abundant gift, undeserved gift, gift that makes everything wrong wondrously right.

In recent years the hymn by John Newton has rightly become very popular:

> Amazing grace—how sweet the sound—
> That saved a wretch like me!
> I once was lost, but now am found,
> Was blind, but now I see.

In some songbooks the second line has been changed to read: "That gave new life to me." But Paul would know that for grace to be amazing it needs to save us from our wretchedness. As in Paul's argument in Romans 1:17–3:28, the first word is the word of grace. In the light of that grace we know that we were lost, were blind; now we rejoice in our being found, in our newfound sight.

God's grace, according to Paul, does two things for humankind. God's grace forgives, passes over, forgets our former sins. God grants unconditional amnesty. God is like a governor who at the last minute gets an appeal to commute our sentence. The governor not only commutes our sentence; the governor declares us innocent, wipes our conviction off the books, sets us free. God's grace justifies, rightwises, makes right—puts us into a right relationship to God so that we acknowledge God as God. God is like the parent who welcomes home the child who has wandered far away, not only forgiving and forgetting, but loving and rejoicing: arms always open, heart always open.

God's grace is given to all of us, or made available to all of us, in the one person Jesus Christ. Here Paul writes especially of Christ's death on the cross as the gift none of us can deserve and none of us should deny. Romans 3:25 packs a very rich and complicated picture of Jesus' death for us into a very few words: "sacrifice, atonement, blood, effective through faith."

Sacrifice: Jesus gave his life for us, and that was the Creator God's gift to us and not Jesus' gift alone.

Atonement: That death also brought us into a right relationship with God: it welcomed us home from the far country. It was God's arms open to us all—on the cross.

Christ's "blood": Not the blood of sacrificial animals in the temple but Christ's blood is what brings us close to God. In his giving of his life we see God's love for us. More than that, in Christ's giving of his life God *does* God's love for us. God acts love. God performs love.

"Effective through faith": Without our faith Jesus seems to us just one more good person who has been martyred. We can admire him, but we do not honor him as God's grace and gift. Through faith we know that a right relationship with God is opened to us all through him.

From Paul's time until now, Christian believers have sought to capture the richness of these terms.

No doctrine and no story can possibly capture the richness of what the cross means for Paul and for us. Many stories help; each shows us a part of what the cross means. I heard a congressman tell of his coming to be a Christian. In World War II he had been caught with some of his company close to enemy lines. A soldier from the other side threw a grenade into their midst, and without a second's hesitation one soldier threw his body on the grenade. He died, and the others lived. The congressman owed his life to that gift, and through that gift he understood that he owed his life and his wholeness to another sacrificial death—Jesus' death on Calvary.

So the grace of God in Jesus Christ forgives our sins and brings us into a right relationship with God's own self. Everyone can receive that grace, be put in a right relationship to God, because everyone can have faith. The law is given to Jews only, but faith is a gift God wishes to give to all of humankind. Grace; Christ; faith. God's gifts to all who will receive.

What seems to be a postscript may be the heart of the matter.

> Then what becomes of boasting? It is excluded. By what law? By that of works? No, but by the law of faith. (3:27)

In this passage, as throughout Romans, Paul has two attitudes toward the law, attitudes that are in tension with each other. In 3:21 Paul says that the righteousness of God has been revealed apart from the law, but that the law attests to that righteousness. The law cannot bring us righteousness, but the law, the Torah, does point to Christ and Christ does bring righteousness. The law is of great value, but it does not bring us into a right relationship with God.

Yet in Romans 3:27 Paul writes of a "law of works." The law of works is the Torah, and despite all its gifts the Torah divides Christian people from one another, because some follow its commands and others do not. Yet the one God intends for all people to have a right relationship to one another and to God. So Torah can't do it. Torah allows some of us to boast and be separate from others. Faith is the gift that unites.

> Or is God the God of Jews only? Is he not the God of Gentiles also? Yes, of Gentiles also, since God is one; and he will justify the circumcised on the ground of faith and the uncircumcised through that same faith. (3:29–30)

Jews and Gentiles, one people, through faith in the one God.

ABRAHAM, JUSTIFIED BY FAITH
Romans 4:1–25

We know that the chapters, verses, and even paragraphs in our texts of the Bible represent decisions made by editors and translators. The earliest manuscripts had no such clues for interpretation, and indeed the last verses of Romans 3 provide the transition to Paul's claim in Romans 4—that Abraham is the first great example of the righteousness of faith. Although the whole chapter holds together beautifully, we can understand the first half of the chapter as discussing the relationship of Abraham's faith to circumcision, and the second half of the chapter as dealing with Abraham's role as father and example for all people—Jews and Gentiles alike.

If one way to read Romans is as a letter about the obedient faith in the one God, in Romans 4 and 5 Paul provides a central working out of that theme. Both Abraham and Jesus show obedient faith, but in Paul's retelling of Abraham's story he stresses faith. In Paul's retelling of Jesus' story he stresses obedience.

Abraham's Faith and Circumcision (Romans 4:1–15)

4:1 What then are we to say was gained by Abraham, our ancestor according to the flesh? 2 For if Abraham was justified by works, he has something to boast about, but not before God. 3 For what does the scripture say? "Abraham believed God, and it was reckoned to him as righteousness." 4 Now to one who works, wages are not reckoned as a gift but as something due. 5 But to one who without works trusts him who justifies the ungodly, such faith is reckoned as righteousness. 6 So also David speaks of the blessedness of those to whom God reckons righteousness apart from works:
7"Blessed are those whose iniquities are forgiven,
and whose sins are covered;
8 blessed is the one against whom the Lord will not reckon sin."
9 Is this blessedness, then, pronounced only on the circumcised, or also on the uncircumcised? We say, "Faith was reckoned to Abraham as righteousness." 10 How then was it reckoned to him? Was it before or after he had been circumcised? It was not after, but before he was circumcised. 11 He received the sign of circumcision as a seal of the righteousness that he had by faith while he was still uncircumcised. The purpose was to make him the ancestor of all who believe without being circumcised and who thus have righteousness reckoned to them, 12 and likewise the ancestor of the circumcised who are not only circumcised but who also follow the example of the faith that our ancestor Abraham had before he was circumcised.
13 For the promise that he would inherit the world did not come to Abraham or to his descendants through the law but through the righteousness of faith. 14 If it is the adherents of the law who are to be the heirs, faith is null

and the promise is void. ¹⁵ For the law brings wrath, but where there is no law, neither is there violation.

We will never know whether Paul came to his great affirmation that we are justified by faith and then was delighted to discover in Abraham the first example of his principle, or whether Paul discovered in Abraham's story not only the clue but the language for his affirmation.

Certainly the story of Abraham gives Paul exactly what he needs. He needs an example of a right relationship to God that does not depend on the law, because he wants that right relationship to be open to law-abiding Jews and to Gentiles without the law. Of course the law, the Torah (the Old Testament), does not give him any examples of people who lived after the law, but it does give him some examples of people who lived before the law. Abraham's case is complicated because he does foreshadow obedience to the law by his willingness to be circumcised. So Paul needs to see how Abraham related to God before his circumcision. Genesis 15:6 gives Paul just the verse he needs, a story of Abraham's complete trust in God's promises. It is this trust that brings him into a right relationship to God, or confirms God's right relationship to him. "Abraham believed God [had faith in God], and it was reckoned to him as righteousness." And this trust is evident *before* Abraham is circumcised, because Abraham is not circumcised until two chapters later, in Genesis 17:23–27.

Three words in the quotation from Genesis 15:6 are especially important for Paul. "Faith" (or "belief") is the word used to talk about the one way in which all people can enter into a just, right relationship with God. We shall see that for Christians that faith is faith in Jesus Christ or in the God who raised Christ from the dead. For Abraham faith is faith in the promises of God, but for Paul it is evident that the God in whom Abraham believes already is the God who promises Jesus Christ.

"Righteousness" (or "justice" or "justification"), we have seen, is the word Paul uses to describe our right relationship to God and by extension our right relationship to one another. Both "righteousness" and "justice" were also used in Habakkuk 2:4, that other verse from the Bible that Paul loves to quote: "The one who is righteous will live by faith" or "The one who is righteous through faith will live" (Rom. 1:17).

"Reckon" (or "account") is the third word that is crucial for Paul in this quotation from Genesis. It is a word we do not use much anymore, but when we call our bank to see how much is left in our account we are asking for a "reckoning," and the "reckoning" tells us how much we're worth in monetary terms. Paul says that God keeps accounts of all of us, reckons our worth. What counts to our account, or confirms our reckoning, is faith.

Abraham's story provides one example of this reckoning. The other example, in Romans 4:6–8, Paul finds in Psalms 32:1–2. (Paul never doubts that the Psalms were written by David, and he therefore introduces the reference by citing David.) Paul's main point in quoting the psalm is to show that God may reckon either sin or righteousness and that blessedness is, for those like Abraham who have righteousness reckoned to them, added to their account. Paul also suggests, by quoting this psalm, what he suggested in Romans 3:25: The righteousness of God in which we are called to live includes the forgiveness of sins, God's unconditional amnesty. Of course for Paul that amnesty to which David points is accomplished in Jesus Christ.

Sometimes when Paul provides a quotation from scripture, he has in mind more than just the verses he cites. That may be the case here, because Psalm 32 in the Greek version of the Old Testament (the Septuagint) ends with this verse, translated by me rather woodenly: "Be glad in the Lord and rejoice, you righteous! And boast, all you who are upright in heart!" Part of what Paul worries about all through Romans, and even at the beginning of this section, is the question, When is it appropriate to boast? And why? Human boasting, about all the good things we do, is not appropriate to the faithful life. It confuses our relationship to God. It makes it seem that our relationship to God is our own doing. Human boasting confuses our relationship with other people, because when I boast I imply that I am better than you—more pious, more ethical, more successful. Such boasting separates us from one another.

Boasting in God, rejoicing in God, being overjoyed by all the good God does—that is entirely appropriate to the Christian life. In Psalm 32 the "righteous"—Paul's favorite word again—are those who boast and rejoice in the Lord. (In the Septuagint this is Psalm 31:11.)

There is one more thing to be said about this "reckoning" or "accounting." Paul wants us to look at the way in which we understand accounting, counting, and keeping score. We may build an account of goods in two ways. One is by working; then if our account is full, we've earned it. That's our wages, our paycheck. But suppose one day, when we have just balanced the checkbook and discovered there's not much left to balance, the bank calls and says, "Your account is full and running over." This is the second way—a gift, a surprise, an amazing grace. For Paul, God's righteousness is gift, surprise, amazing grace. So when Genesis says that

Abraham had righteousness reckoned to him, Genesis says that Abraham got a full account as a gift. Surprise!

Notice that Paul's argument isn't a straightforward argument like so many sermons we hear or books we write. "Let me tell you about righteousness, and then about faith, and then about reckoning. Let me interpret Genesis and then interpret the Psalm." Paul links his argument by repeating words and discussing images and talking about how they relate to each other.

The paragraphs are so dense and compact that it is hard to find a key sentence, but if we had to find a punchline, this would be my candidate: "Now to one who works, wages are not reckoned as a gift but as something due. But to one who without works trusts him [God] who justifies the ungodly, such faith is reckoned as righteousness" (Rom. 4:4–5). When Paul says that Abraham provides an example for the ungodly, he doesn't mean that Abraham was a notorious sinner. He means that Abraham had faith before there was any law. He had faith before people started practicing circumcision and all the ways we try to work our way into God's favor. He is therefore an example for all of us who cannot figure out any good way to get ourselves to God (we are ungodly) but who trust that in Jesus Christ God has gotten to us (we have faith).

Verses 9–13 provide the transition to the great claim of the last part of the chapter, that what God did in Abraham is an example and indeed a source of righteousness for all of us. Because Abraham was reckoned righteous before he was circumcised, he can be the ancestor not just of Jews but of Gentiles. Notice that Abraham who is "our ancestor according to the flesh" in 4:1 becomes just "our ancestor" in 4:12. Abraham is forerunner and forefather no longer for Jews alone but for Gentiles, too, because his example does not depend on his Jewishness, his circumcision.

In the fall of 1993 when the governments of Israel and Jordan began talking about a permanent peace between Jewish and Arab neighbors, Shimon Peres, the foreign minister of Israel, said: "We have a river in common and a desert in common and a father in common—Abraham." The claim that Abraham is the father of Isaac's descendants (the Jews) and Ishmael's descendants (the Arabs) is clearly based on the Bible. Peres took that biblical claim as the sign that Jews and Arabs should be reconciled to each other.

Paul thinks that the Bible also says that Jews and Gentiles have Abraham as a common father, not because Abraham sired us all biologically, but because we can share his faith. In the first century Paul proposed a reconciliation as amazing as the reconciliation Israelis and Arabs are beginning to work out for the twenty-first century. Paul announced that in Abraham Jews and Gentiles are reconciled *through faith*. The church is a family that breaks down the old walls of history and tradition and custom and ethnic background. It is God's family and Abraham's family, too.

Then in Romans 4:13–15 Paul draws one of his great dividing lines. On the one side is the law, on the other faith. You can't have both; you have to choose. If faith is what counts—as Genesis and Habakkuk insist—then obedience to the regulations of the old covenant does not make us righteous. Law brings wrath, says Paul, pointing ahead to themes he will discuss more fully in Romans 6 and 7.

Abraham's Faith and Our Faith
(Romans 4:16–25)

4:16 **For this reason it depends on faith, in order that the promise may rest on grace and be guaranteed to all his descendants, not only to the adherents of the law but also to those who share the faith of Abraham (for he is the father of all of us, 17 as it is written, "I have made you the father of many nations")—in the presence of the God in whom he believed, who gives life to the dead and calls into existence the things that do not exist. 18 Hoping against hope, he believed that he would become "the father of many nations," according to what was said, "So numerous shall your descendants be." 19 He did not weaken in faith when he considered his own body, which was already as good as dead (for he was about a hundred years old), or when he considered the barrenness of Sarah's womb. 20 No distrust made him waver concerning the promise of God, but he grew strong in his faith as he gave glory to God, 21 being fully convinced that God was able to do what he had promised. 22 Therefore his faith "was reckoned to him as righteousness." 23 Now the words, "it was reckoned to him," were written not for his sake alone, 24 but for ours also. It will be reckoned to us who believe in him who raised Jesus our Lord from the dead, 25 who was handed over to death for our trespasses and was raised for our justification.**

It is not quite clear why the NRSV places the sentence that connects Romans 4:16 with Romans 4:17 in parentheses— "for he is the father of all of us." We have see that this claim is at the very heart of what Paul is saying: Abraham "is the father of all of us, as it is written, 'I have made you the father of many nations.' "

Romans 4:16 again shows the way in which Abraham is the ancestor of all who have faith, Jew and Gentile alike. He is our father because we share his faith. In Romans 4:17 Paul quotes Genesis 17:5, where Abraham is still not circumcised. The quotation means two things at once: (1) "I have made you the father of many nations" and (2) "I have made you the father of many Gentiles." Because Abraham is father of many nations, his parental role includes all who have faith, Jews and Gentiles alike.

The content of Abraham's faith is related to his confidence in the promise that he and Sarah will have a son, the promise fulfilled in the birth of Isaac. The God who makes that promise is the God "who gives life to the dead and calls into existence the things that do not exist" (Rom. 4:17). In terms of the immediate story of Abraham and Sarah this reminds us that God provides them with a son, though in terms of their potential for pro-creation they are as good as dead. The verse reminds us that God brings forth something from nothing, a child from barrenness. In terms of the larger story of God's dealing with us, Abraham foreshadows faith in res-urrection and in creation, or in creation and new creation. Paul has already affirmed faith in God as creator in Romans 1. He will affirm faith in God as redeemer through Christ's resurrection, especially in Romans 5 and 8. Though Paul does not explicitly say that Abraham is the first Christian, Abraham believes in the God who does just what Christians know God does: creates and redeems. (Paul in fact improves Abraham's story some-what over the Genesis version. Anyone reading the story in Genesis 15—17 needs to take it on faith that when it came to Abraham, "No distrust made him waver concerning the promise of God" [Rom. 4:20].)

Paul tells us about the God in whom faith believes. He also tells us what faith looks like. Faith is complete trust in the God who does what God promises. It is contrasted to distrust and to wavering.

Now it is clear why Abraham is our ancestor in the faith. Just as he lived in complete trust in the one who creates and redeems, we are invited to trust "in him who raised Jesus our Lord from the dead" (Rom. 4:24). Note that just as Abraham's faith is not so much belief in the promise as trust in the one who promises, so our faith is not *that* God raised Jesus from the dead but *in* God who raised Jesus from the dead.

Jesus is "our Lord" just because he was "handed over to death for our trespasses." Again Paul reminds us that righteousness, right relationship to God, is in part God's unconditional amnesty declared on our sins. That amnesty is declared and enacted in the cross. Jesus is "our Lord" because he was "raised for our justification" or "rightwising" or "being made righ-teous." With Paul it is often misleading to try to divide his claims of faith neatly, as if crucifixion accomplished forgiveness and resurrection accom-plished new life. Cross and resurrection are the way in which God brings us into a right relationship with God's self and with one another.

Paul has Abraham believing everything a Christian should believe, save perhaps that Jesus is the fulfillment of all the promises God gave to Abraham. Abraham has faith in the God who justifies the ungodly, creates everything out of nothing, and gives life to the dead. For Paul the God who is God is the God who does just exactly these things. These are the great gifts that are so far beyond our imagining that to lay hold of these gifts in faith is to lay hold of life. Apart from these gifts there is no life, but with these gifts, no one could ask for any richer life than God provides. By laying hold of these gifts Abraham becomes father of us all.

Now the rightness, righteousness, justification that God reckoned to Abraham, God also reckons to everyone who has faith, whether Jew or Gentile. Just as Abraham's account is filled up by God's good gift, unmerited, unearned, so by what God has done in Jesus Christ our account is filled up, full measure and running over.

Notice how Paul reads the Old Testament, his Bible. He knows full well that Abraham was not part of the Christian church and did not live in the first century. Yet Abraham's story becomes a story for first-century Gentiles and Jews as they move toward faith. In the same way Abraham's story and Paul's story and the story of the Roman Christians seeking to live with one another in the light of the gospel become our stories, though the issues change and the language seems old-fashioned.

Like the Jews and Gentiles of the churches at Rome, we contemporary Christians try desperately to find ways to reckon ourselves right with God and better than one another. Theological and denominational ties, occupation, wealth, lifestyle—we wear them all on our sleeves as if our credentials might somehow make us a force to be reckoned with.

God reckons that all our reckoning is in vain. God is always astonishing us with gifts immeasurably more than the wages we strive to earn. We work for security and receive joy. We work for fame and receive love. We work for prestige and receive boundless, unmerited kindness from our God. Abraham and Sarah, muddling along, little dreamed that they would be given a son. We, muddling along, often forget that we have been given God's son. God brings creation out of nothing and Christ out of the grave and our lives out of the kind of dullness or frenzy that comes when we spend each night counting up our own accomplishments and reckoning our own worth.

We set out wanting to boast in ourselves, and either we find little to boast about and fall into despair, or we pretend there is much to boast about and turn ourselves into our own gods, every bit as silly as the birds and cats the Gentiles worshiped in Paul's day. But the God who is God acts for us in Jesus Christ and gives us something to boast about, someone to boast in. We boast in God who brings something out of nothing and gives life to the dead, through Jesus Christ, God's great reckoning for our sake and the world's.

3. Living in Hope
Romans 5—8

Romans 5—8 is like a circle. Romans 5 begins with an affirmation of the hope under which we live as people who know that we are brought into a right relationship with God by our faith in Jesus Christ. Romans 8 draws the vision of what we hope for, in even greater detail. In Romans 6—7, however, Paul looks at questions and objections to his gospel, before bringing us back full circle to the affirmation of good news. The structure can be shown in a kind of outline, using the first verses of each section to show how Paul moves from affirmation to question to question to affirmation:

Affirmation: "Therefore, since we are justified by faith, we have peace with God through our Lord Jesus Christ." (Romans 5)

Question: "What then are we to say? Should we continue in sin in order that grace may abound?" (Romans 6)

Question: "Do you not know, brothers and sisters . . . that the law is binding on a person only during that person's lifetime?" (Romans 7)

Affirmation: "There is therefore now no condemnation of those who are in Christ Jesus." (Romans 8)

ACCESS TO GRACE
Romans 5:1–21

Paul's affirmation of hope in Romans 5 can be divided into two sections, or moves. In the first section he explains his claim that it is through God's grace in Jesus Christ that we have access to God. In the second section he shows how Christ makes that access possible by being obedient where Adam was only disobedient.

Access to Jesus Christ (Romans 5:1–11)

5:1 **Therefore, since we are justified by faith, we have peace with God through our Lord Jesus Christ,** 2 **through whom we have obtained access to** this grace in which we stand; and we boast in our hope of sharing the glory of God. [3] And not only that, but we also boast in our sufferings, knowing that suffering produces endurance, [4] and endurance produces character, and character produces hope, [5] and hope does not disappoint us, because God's love has been poured into our hearts through the Holy Spirit that has been given to us.

[6] For while we were still weak, at the right time Christ died for the ungodly. [7] Indeed, rarely will anyone die for a righteous person—though perhaps for a good person someone might actually dare to die. [8] But God proves his love for us in that while we were still sinners Christ died for us. [9] Much more surely then, now that we have been justified by his blood, will we be saved through him from the wrath of God. [10] For if while we were enemies, we were reconciled to God through the death of his Son, much more surely, having been reconciled, will we be saved by his life. [11] But more than that, we even boast in God through our Lord Jesus Christ, through whom we have now received reconciliation.

Paul has just been writing about Abraham as the father of us all—in faith (4:1–25). Now he underlines what has been evident all along. Not even our father Abraham can provide faith for us. It is through Jesus Christ that we are given faith. Furthermore, the faith we are given is our faith *in* Jesus Christ. The faith that unites us to Abraham is our faith in Jesus Christ. Abraham is our father in faith because, for Paul, Abraham is the first Christian. He is the first person to have faith in the God who creates and raises from the dead—the God who is revealed in Jesus Christ.

Paul now tells the Romans about the results of that right relationship we have to God in Jesus Christ. Through faith we have peace with God and we have access to the grace in which we stand.

"Grace" and "peace," we remember, are the two words Paul used in his greeting to the Romans (Rom. 1:7). "Peace" is the English translation (through Greek) of the Hebrew word *shalom*. When Paul writes that we have peace with God, he means that we are delivered from God's wrath. We live with a kind of negative peace, the absence of conflict with God. We enjoy the amnesty declared in Jesus Christ. Paul also means that we enter into a relationship of wholeness with God. We love the one God wholly and our lives find their fullness, their fulfillment, in that relationship. We have positive peace, the new life brought about in Jesus Christ.

"Grace" often refers to that gracious act of God in Jesus Christ, the time when God reconciled us to God's self. Here, however, grace is a place, a sphere, the arena in which we live and move and have our being. Grace is like the Promised Land into which Joshua led the children of Israel. Grace is like the home we long for. We speak not only of a gracious act but of the "state of grace," like the state of Connecticut, a realm in which we live.

John Newton's wonderful hymn catches both aspects of the term:

> Amazing grace—how sweet the sound—
> That saved a wretch like me!

(Grace as an act of God, taking place in time)

> Through many dangers, toils, and snares,
> I have already come;
> 'Tis grace has brought me safe thus far,
> And grace will lead me home.

(Grace as place, space, the sphere in which we act and in which God acts upon us)

Like peace, "grace" is both amnesty for old sins and the promise of new life. Like peace, grace is a gift from God. Like peace, grace is given and guaranteed in Jesus Christ—to all who have faith.

The image of Christ as the access to grace brings to mind other images, both new and old. The image of access reminds us of the picture of Christ as the bread of life, whose word nourishes us and gives to us eternal life (John 6). The image reminds us too of the picture of Christ as the living water delivering us from the thirst of our souls (John 4). One student with whom I discussed this passage also suggested that Christ is like the ATM card we put in the bank machine, providing access to the resources we need for our lives.

Yet another image may help. I spent much of one morning trying to telephone a friend in Germany, but I had the wrong access code for the city where he lived. When at last I found the right code and dialed the correct three numbers before his phone number, there he was. We sometimes search for God, not remembering that Jesus Christ is God's way of access. Knowing Christ, we find God close and clear. Of course these images are a little "materialistic," but "bread" and "water" are material, too. They can point to deeper realities, and so perhaps can the plastic card that provides access to our account and the telephone code that provides access to my friend. This is especially the case if we remember that what we have in our account is not what we have earned but the abundant goodness that God has accounted, reckoned, counted for us (as in Rom. 4:4–5). What we have access to is the kindness and generosity of God.

Then in Romans 5:2 Paul brings us back to his old word for the way people live: "boasting." We all boast of something, Paul suggests. Perhaps we boast of ourselves, our accomplishments, our possessions, our piety. All of that boasting is idolatry. Perhaps we boast of God, rejoice in God. In Jesus Christ we learn to boast as we should—"in our hope of sharing the glory of God." Of course it's not *our* hope we boast in. That would be no more faithful than boasting in our piety or our IQ. We boast in God. God gives us hope, and God's glory is what we hope for, what we boast in.

Surely in part Paul here recalls the words of Jeremiah 9:23–24:

> Thus says the LORD: Do not let the wise boast in their wisdom, do not let the mighty boast in their might, do not let the wealthy boast in their wealth; but let those who boast boast in this, that they understand and know me, that I am the LORD; I act with steadfast love, justice, and righteousness in the earth, for in these things I delight, says the LORD.

What we are called to boast in, glory in, is the glory of God. We have seen that for Paul God is the one who acts with "righteousness in the earth."

Paul tells the Romans that even though we do not yet fully know the glory of God, we see signs of that glory in our present situation. Oddly enough, the evidence for hope is not our success but our suffering. Remember that some Roman Christians had just returned from long exile from their homes and livelihood, and, for the most part, Christians, both Jewish and Gentile, were not among the few powerful and wealthy in Rome. Before long, persecution would increase among them, and of course Paul himself had already known persecution aplenty (see 2 Cor. 11:22–29).

Notice how different this is from much of the so-called gospel of success today. "If you want proof that you will have glory," say the preachers, "notice how much you are prospering now." We can see why this would not work for Paul. Prosperity can all too easily lead us to boast in ourselves, and that turns us from our boasting in God and from the hope of glory that comes with that boasting.

The move from suffering to hope takes us through several stages. It is not so much that each of these stages follows the other. It is rather that they are all bound together as part of the faithful life. The move proceeds like this:

Suffering produces endurance. (The skin scarred over a wound is stronger than the skin never touched by injury. The soul that survives suffering learns to endure.)

Endurance produces character. (The practice of endurance is itself character. Character is what *characterizes* us. To have character is to have integrity. It is to have spiritual strength not just for the occasional moment at a time but over the long haul.)

Character produces hope. (We might have thought that optimism produces hope, or good luck produces hope. But the person who had endured, the person of character, is the person who lives with hope.)

The hope of a person of integrity is not simply the cheery belief that all's for the best despite all evidence to the contrary. The hope of a person of integrity is the hope that emerges because that person has lived through the worst and not lost faith. That hope finds its proof not in a full checking account or promotion or even in robust good health but in the love of God, which the Spirit daily confirms in the lives of those who endure suffering boldly.

One of the most remarkable Christians I have known lived most of her adult life with suffering. While her husband was still young, he took seriously ill and became an invalid. She was left to care for him and their five children, and to make a living for the family. She was not in the best of health herself. Yet those who knew her testified that she was a person of strength and integrity and kindness: a person of character.

At the memorial service after she died, I heard a poem read that had been one of her favorites. It is an anonymous poem that catches something of the hope that character produced:

> If but one message I may leave behind,
> One single word of comfort for my kind,
> It would be this,
> O brother, sister, friend,
> Whatever life may bring or God may send,
> take heart and wait.
>
> Despair may tangle darkly at your feet
> And hope once cool and sweet
> Be lost. But suddenly above a hill
> A heavenly lamp set on a heavenly sill
> Will shine for you
> And point the way to go.
>
> How well I know,
> For I have waited through the dark,
> And I have seen a star rise in the blackest sky, repeatedly,
> It has not failed me yet,
> And I have learned

God never will forget
To light his lamp.
If we but wait for it,
It will be lit.

Romans 5:5 is the only place where Paul so closely connects God's love
with the gift of the Spirit. Whatever else God's Spirit does for us, says
Paul, the Spirit provides God's love. The Spirit *is* God's love poured out
in our hearts.

If the Spirit is God's love poured out in our hearts, the cross is God's
love poured out for the whole creation. Paul next makes a comparison between what might be humanly possible and what God has done. It is humanly possible that someone heroic might give up his or her life for some
deserving person. Such human activity is *rare* enough that we hold cere-
monies and give medals to honor those who behave so heroically. And
such human activity is *common* enough that we actually do hold such cer-
emonies and award such medals.

What seems beyond even human heroism is the possibility that one
might give up one's life for someone who could hardly be called deserving, someone we have no natural or family reason to love. (All this is picture and parable. What God has done in Jesus Christ is larger even than
Paul's comparisons.) The death of Jesus Christ on the cross shows God's
love for us when we were:

weak
ungodly
still sinners

When Paul uses this language, he is not talking about three different prob-
lems God had to overcome. He is talking about our basic problem in three
different ways.

We were weak. That is, we didn't have the strength to make ourselves
right with God, to enter into a right relationship with God.
We were ungodly. That is, because we didn't have the strength to make
ourselves right with God we threw up our hands and settled for
trusting in ourselves.
We were still sinners. That is, we were separate from God. We were
unable to overcome that separation by our own achievement.

Paul will talk a good deal more about this sinfulness, weakness, ungodliness in chapters 6 and 7 of this letter. And all these descriptions recall the story of Adam. Adam was too weak to obey God's command, too ungodly to look God in the face, and so much a sinner that he hid from the grace that could have redeemed him. Of course Paul thinks Adam also sounds a good deal like us. Even if we try our hardest to make ourselves right with God, that rightness is not something we can do for ourselves. So we are apt to give up and say we don't care anyway. And the less we care, the farther we fall into sin. For example:

"I'm disappointed in you," says the mother of the unruly child.

"I'll make a funny face for you," says the child. Or run around the room. Or tell you a joke. But none of that makes right the wrong.

"Well, if you're going to be mean to me, I'll be mean to you," says the child. But that just makes the wrong worse. The truth is that, finally, it will take the mother's forgiving—not excusing but forgiving—to make it right.

"While we were still weak, at the right time Christ died for the ungodly." It was the right time, just because we *were* weak and we were ungodly and we were sinners. It was the right time because time had run out, as time is always running out. It was the right time because each day begins with both the news that time is running out and the better news that this is a good time, the right time, to hear the gospel.

That is good news for Paul, and should be good news for us as well. As much as we like to think that we are the godly and that those other people (with their odd beliefs or their odd behavior or their odd dress or their poverty) are the ungodly, the truth is that Adam's story is our story. We have all sinned and fallen short of the glory of God. If Christ did not die for the ungodly, what hope is there for us?

Put it the other way around: Christ died for us! It is not just that he taught us good things or healed the sick. He gave his life. Who is good enough to deserve that? Before such a gift the most pious of us is ungodly, and in the light of such bounty the strongest of us is weak. All have sinned because every one of us has fallen short of that astonishing glory.

> When I survey the wondrous cross
> On which the Prince of glory died,
> My richest gain I count but loss,
> And pour contempt on all my pride.

Now again Paul moves from the good news of what God has done to the good news of what God will do—from our faith to our hope. We have been justified . . . we shall be saved. We have been reconciled . . . we shall be saved. That is, our present confidence in God will bear further fruit, because whatever wrath and judgment God will visit on the creation will not destroy us. For Paul the answer to the question "Are you saved?" is always "Not yet." But Christians can say: "We have been reconciled, brought close to God in the cross." We are like the disobedient child whose mother finally takes him in her arms, to chasten and forgive. We are like Adam and Eve, whom God followed into the wilderness.

And because God loves us (we are reconciled) and will love us for eternity (we shall be saved) we can do what Paul calls us to do again and again. We can boast! Of course we do not boast in ourselves, weak ungodly sinners. We boast in God through our Lord Jesus Christ.

I have suggested that Paul has had the story of Adam in the garden in the back of his mind up until now in this chapter. Now Paul brings Adam to the forefront, downstage, for us all to consider.

Disobedient Adam, Obedient Christ
(Romans 5:12–21)

5:12 Therefore, just as sin came into the world through one man, and death came through sin, and so death spread to all because all have sinned— [13] sin was indeed in the world before the law, but sin is not reckoned where there is no law. [14] Yet death exercised dominion from Adam to Moses, even over those whose sins were not like the transgression of Adam who is a type of the one who was to come.

[15] But the free gift is not like the trespass. For if the many died through the one man's trespass, much more surely have the grace of God and the free gift in the grace of the one man, Jesus Christ, abounded for the many. [16] And the free gift is not like the effect of the one man's sin. For the judgment following one trespass brought condemnation, but the free gift following many trespasses brings justification. [17] If, because of the one man's trespass, death exercised dominion through that one, much more surely will those who receive the abundance of grace and the free gift of righteousness exercise dominion in life through the one man, Jesus Christ.

[18] Therefore just as one man's trespass led to condemnation for all, so one man's act of righteousness leads to justification and life for all. [19] For just as by the one man's disobedience the many were made sinners, so by the one man's obedience the many will be made righteous. [20] But law came in, with the result that the trespass multiplied; but where sin increased, grace abounded all the more, [21] so that, just as sin exercised dominion in death, so grace might also exercise dominion through justification leading to eternal life through Jesus Christ our Lord.

For many of the people to whom Paul wrote, there were great representative figures who helped them understand who they were. We can understand this by using Abraham Lincoln as an example. It has been said that Abraham Lincoln was every American grown a little taller. Certainly we love to read and tell Lincoln's story because we see in it those virtues we think we have—or wish we had—as Americans. Paul has already suggested to the Roman church that Abraham could be such a representative figure, both for Jews and for Gentiles, because Abraham had faith in God, and such faith is a possibility and gift for every human being.

Now Paul talks about two other representative figures, Adam and Christ. They represent equal and opposite possibilities. More accurately, they represent opposite and unequal possibilities:

Adam represents disobedience, which leads to condemnation.

Jesus Christ represents obedience, which leads to justification and life.

And for Paul their stories are also *our* story. In an age devoted to storytelling, it would cause something of a stir if a Christian were told to tell her story and she told it this way:

In the garden, I disobeyed God and received the just punishment for my disobedience. On Calvary, I obeyed God and was restored to a right relationship to God. That is my story in its most important features. The rest fills in the details.

Yet while Paul loves to fill in the details of his story (see Galatians 1 or Philippians 3 or 2 Corinthians 11), he also claims that in fact the most important features of our story are these: In Adam (or like Adam) we have been disobedient. In Christ we have been forgiven that disobedience and brought into a right—obedient—relationship with God.

Paul assumes that the Roman Christians know the story of Adam's disobedience (we can find the story in Genesis 2 and 3). God gives Adam only one commandment: "You may freely eat of every tree of the garden; but of the tree of the knowledge of good and evil you shall not eat, for in the day that you eat of it you shall die" (Gen. 2:16–17). Of course that one commandment includes a whole host of meanings: You shall honor God as God by obeying God (and as the story later says, by not trying to eat a fruit that will make you like God). You shall rejoice in the much that has been given you and not go lusting after the little that has not. Much of the Ten Commandments is already foreshadowed by this one commandment. Adam dis-

obeys the one commandment and death enters the world. Death does not
enter right on the spot. Adam doesn't drop dead right then. But mortality
enters the world. Adam disobeyed; so do we. Adam will die, so will we.

Jesus does just the opposite. He obeys. (I don't think Paul has the temp-
tations of Christ in the wilderness in mind here, as John Milton did when
he contrasted Adam and Christ in his two epics, *Paradise Lost* and *Paradise
Regained.* For Paul, the time of Christ's obedience is always the cross, and
we remember that we got to this passage by talking about how Christ died
at the right time for the ungodly.) Through Christ's obedience, eternal
life enters the world. Life does not enter right on the spot. Christ is not
rescued from the cross, and we shall not escape death. But on the third day
he rose again, and our resurrection, too, is promised as a gift.

Adam and Christ are opposite but not equal. They are not equal because Adam and Christ are not equal. Adam is the first human being.
Christ is Adam's son, but also son of God. They are not equal because
what Christ does is so much greater than what Adam does. Adam gets us
all toward death, and that is fairly impressive. Christ brings us all to life,
and that is beyond words to tell.

Many rabbis in Paul's time, and since, liked to argue "from the lesser
to the greater." Jesus does this: "If you then, who are evil, know how to
give good gifts to your children, how much more will the heavenly Father
give the Holy Spirit to those who ask him!" (Luke 11:13). Paul uses this
kind of argument in Romans again and again:

> If the many died through the one man's trespass, much more surely have
> the grace of God and the free gift in the grace of the one man, Jesus Christ,
> abounded for the many. (5:15)

> The judgment . . . brought condemnation . . . the free gift . . . brings justi-
> fication. (5:16)

> If, because of the one man's trespass, death exercised dominion, . . . much
> more surely will those who receive the abundance of grace . . . exercise do-
> minion in life through the one man, Jesus Christ. (5:17)

Our song works well again: "Amazing grace—how sweet the sound—
that saved a wretch like me." We know real wretchedness, of course, but
it is nothing compared to grace, which is not only real, it is amazing.

Of course another issue now begins to intrude on Paul's discussion of
Christ and Adam, as it did on his discussion of Abraham. How does obedience relate to the law, how does righteousness relate to the law? Paul provides one clue that looks back to the beginning of the letter: "sin was in-

deed in the world before the law, but sin is not reckoned where there is no law" (5:13). Remember, in the discussion of righteousness being "reckoned" to Abraham (Rom. 4:1–15) I suggested that Paul has one image of God's dealing with us that sounds a little like an account book. What gets counted for us? Here Paul hints that sin doesn't get counted as severely where there is no law. It is one thing to do the wrong thing without being told the right. It is another thing to break an explicit commandment. Paul begins to hint at this rather complicated answer in Romans 5:20: "But law came in, with the result that the trespass multiplied." We shall need to look at what Paul means by that as he answers questions about his position in Romans 6 and 7. Yet the law still does not even the odds between disobedience and obedience: "But law came in, with the result that the trespass multiplied; but where sin increased, grace abounded all the more."

This section of Romans ends by finding yet one more way to show the great contrast between life in Adam and life in Christ. How much they are alike! How much they are unlike! How much more is Christ! ". . . so that, just as sin exercised dominion in death, so grace might also exercise dominion through justification leading to eternal life through Jesus Christ our Lord" (5:21).

On the one side of the great divide there is sin that leads to death. On the other side of the great divide there is grace that leads to life. Jesus Christ is the great dividing point in history and in every person's history. God's good gift, overwhelming bounty, grace, righteousness are given us in Jesus Christ. When we come to Jesus Christ, or when we receive God's righteousness, we also receive the promise of eternal life. "Eternal life" is not a phrase Paul uses very often, but it surely means both the promise of life beyond death and the quality of rich, faithful life right now.

The old primer used by children to learn English in colonial New England made a point rather like Paul's point in the saying: "In Adam's fall, we sinned all." Paul's greater point, however, is that in Christ's obedience we are all brought into a right relationship with God, both for this life and for the life to come.

Abraham and Paul give us the great picture of Paul's call to the obedience of faith. In Abraham we see faithful obedience, in Jesus obedient faith.

OBJECTIONS AND RESPONSE
Romans 6:1–7:25

In Romans 6 and 7 Paul responds to questions that he imagines the Roman Christians might want to ask about his claim that in Jesus Christ, God justifies us by grace through faith. Some of these questions may seem artificial. Paul works like the preacher who raises just the question he needs so that he can provide the answer he believes. Some of the questions, however, may reflect Paul's own experience in other churches. For instance, some Corinthian Christians apparently believed in a doctrine of grace that freed them from ethical responsibility. They might as well sin the more since grace all the more abounded. Their motto seems to be: "All things are lawful." To which Paul replies: "But not all things are beneficial" (1 Cor. 6:12). His response to his imagined questioners in Romans addresses even more fully and directly the mistaken notion that God's grace frees us from moral responsibility.

Would More Sin Lead to More Grace?
(Romans 6:1–14)

6:1 **What then are we to say? Should we continue in sin in order that grace may abound?** [2] **By no means! How can we who died to sin go on living in it?** [3] **Do you not know that all of us who have been baptized into Christ Jesus were baptized into his death?** [4] **Therefore we have been buried with him by baptism into death, so that, just as Christ was raised from the dead by the glory of the Father, so we too might walk in newness of life.**

[5] **For if we have been united with him in a death like his, we will certainly be united with him in a resurrection like his.** [6] **We know that our old self was crucified with him so that the body of sin might be destroyed, and we might no longer be enslaved to sin.** [7] **For whoever has died is freed from sin.** [8] **But if we have died with Christ, we believe that we will also live with him.** [9] **We know that Christ, being raised from the dead, will never die again; death no longer has dominion over him.** [10] **The death he died, he died to sin, once for all; but the life he lives, he lives to God.** [11] **So you also must consider yourselves dead to sin and alive to God in Christ Jesus.**

[12] **Therefore, do not let sin exercise dominion in your mortal bodies, to make you obey their passions.** [13] **No longer present your members to sin as instruments of wickedness, but present yourselves to God as those who have been brought from death to life, and present your members to God as instruments of righteousness.** [14] **For sin will have no dominion over you, since you are not under law but under grace.**

The notion that the goodness of grace frees us from responsible obedience is still with us. We ignore questions of economic and social justice because "the gospel is not really about that." We excuse our own tendency to spend our time and energy on people just like ourselves because, after all, the attempt to be more inclusive is just a kind of works righteousness.

We think that because our hearts belong to Jesus, our bodies, our checkbooks, our votes, and our property values belong to us.

Paul does not think that grace frees us from responsible obedience. Grace shapes us into responsible and obedient people.

I remember from my childhood and confess from my own parenting the frequent use of a speech that went something like this: "I don't understand how you could do such a thing. This isn't like you at all." Paul argues with the Romans that as appealing as sin may be, being sinful isn't like them at all. He uses three reminders to help them recall who they really are, and therefore what kind of attitude and behavior *is* "like them."

Haven't You Been Baptized?

It seems likely that the baptism Paul practiced and that he assumed among the Romans included lowering the candidate into the water and bringing the Christian up again. In this way baptism took on the shape of Christ's own death, descent into the tomb, and resurrection on the third day. For Paul baptism is not a kind of picture of who we are in Christ; baptism *is* who we are in Christ. Just as Christ raised on the third day will not ever die again, so we, raised from the baptismal waters, will not fall again into our love of sin. Paul, of course, knows that sometimes Christians do fall into sin, but when we do that we aren't being our true selves at all, but somebody else.

Do You Belong to Adam or to Christ?

Adam, after all, is the one who followed the path of disobedience toward death. Christ is the one who followed the path of obedience toward life. In the last part of Romans 5, Paul has just shown the Romans that we all belong to Christ and not to Adam, and that one day the whole creation will belong to Christ as well. Christ, in whom we live, is the one who is fully present and fully obedient to God. We too are invited, called, into full obedience. More than that, God counts on our obedience as Christ's own people—not Adam's people anymore.

Of Which Age Are You a Citizen?

Everything Paul writes presupposes that in Jesus Christ the whole of history is shifting from the "old age" to the new age. In the old age people sinned, needed the law, and faced God's wrath. In the new age, by grace, people are brought into a right relationship with God. The new age is the age of faith, not law. It is the age of life, not death. And it is the age of obedience, not sin. It is a little like the struggling American colonies when they weren't colonies anymore but a nation. Should they crown a king and bow down to him, or was that simply a mark of citizenship in an old age? In this new age, this new nation, was everything to happen quite differently?

Of course Paul can't conceive of people who never bow to anyone. For Paul all of us belong to some power. Someone has dominion, rule, or authority over us. In the old age we bowed down to sin, a dotty and presumptuous ruler requiring outlandish signs of loyalty and taxing our very souls. In the new age we bow down to the God of Jesus Christ, who asks total obedience but who gives total grace, goodness, and uprightness. "Love God and do as you will," said Augustine, the fifth-century bishop and theologian, in one of his seemingly outrageous sayings that show us the gospel. Augustine means that those who truly love God choose to do what is right. Paul would agree—trusting that if the God we love is really God, what we will to do will be God's will.

When Paul tells the Romans who we really are—baptized, Christ's people, living in the new age—he talks a good deal about life. I suggested earlier that for Paul "eternal life" is both the promise of life beyond death and the quality of a rich, full, lively life here and now.

A main theme of Romans 6:1–14 is that we are to claim our rightful citizenship in the new age. Another theme is Paul's strong affirmation of the life we receive through faith.

Right here and now, says Paul, we have newness of life. That means that we live out of faith and obedience and not out of sin and fear. However, says Paul, we do not yet have Christ's resurrection life. We *will* certainly be united with him in a resurrection like his (Rom. 6:5). I have suggested that Paul may be remembering his not-always-cheerful relationship with the Christians in Corinth when he writes this letter. Sometimes it seems that the Corinthian Christians believed that they were already living the resurrection life, and this meant that they were not very prudent or responsible about issues like sexuality or the relationships between wealthy and poor people. They believed that in the resurrection they wouldn't have to worry about those things. Paul believes that in Christ we have newness of life, but it's still newness of life in this world, before the final resurrection of the dead. In Romans 12—15 he will discuss at some length some of the very practical things we do as people who have been baptized and raised to a rich, full obedient life, but not yet to the heavenly places.

Of course Paul's claims about our identity have implications for our behavior. We are supposed to live out our loyalties, not pledging allegiance to sin but pledging allegiance to God. Pledging allegiance, of course, is not just putting our hands over our hearts but putting heart and hand together in God's service.

Verse 14, the last verse of our section, ends this section rather surprisingly. We would expect Paul to write: "For sin will have no dominion over you, since you are not under sin but under grace." What Paul says, however, is "For sin will have no dominion over you since you are not under *law* but under grace." Of course Paul doesn't know he's ending what would later be called a section of his letter. He intended the sentence to move us into the next paragraph and the next objection he needs to answer.

Why Not Go Ahead and Sin? (Romans 6:15–23)

6:15 **What then? Should we sin because we are not under law but under grace? By no means!** [16] **Do you not know that if you present yourselves to anyone as obedient slaves, you are slaves of the one whom you obey, either of sin, which leads to death, or of obedience, which leads to righteousness?** [17] **But thanks be to God that you, having once been slaves of sin, have become obedient from the heart to the form of teaching to which you were entrusted,** [18] **and that you, having been set free from sin, have become slaves of righteousness.** [19] **I am speaking in human terms because of your natural limitations. For just as you once presented your members as slaves to impurity and to greater and greater iniquity, so now present your members as slaves to righteousness for sanctification.**

[20] **When you were slaves of sin, you were free in regard to righteousness.** [21] **So what advantage did you then get from the things of which you are now ashamed? The end of those things is death.** [22] **But now that you have been freed from sin and enslaved to God, the advantage you get is sanctification. The end is eternal life.** [23] **For the wages of sin is death, but the free gift of God is eternal life in Christ Jesus our Lord.**

Slavery

We cannot think of slavery as having anything good about it at all. This conviction of ours is nurtured by a long history of seeing how awful slavery can be, how awful slavery is by definition.

Yet if we can use our imaginations for a few minutes, we may be able to get closer to what Paul wants the Romans to understand. The idea of the rugged individualist that is so dear to us doesn't really figure in Paul's thinking at all. We have already seen in Paul's discussion of Abraham and Adam that Paul thinks of people as finding their meaning partly in where they belong. Family, community of faith, nation, ancestors—all provide definition for Paul of who we are. That is why the new definition of who we are is so important to him; we are *in* Christ.

One way of talking about belonging is to talk about slavery. I belong to the one who masters me. Paul knows full well that there are masters who demean, but—odd as it may sound—he also believes that there are masters who free. There are loyalties that liberate. Remember that Paul has been talking about life—fullness of life now and the promise of life in the resurrection. A master who provides life is master indeed; a master who deals death is just one more of the usual round of tyrants.

So again we have one of Paul's great contrasts. On the one side, our master can be sin. And of course sin is the greatest tyrant of all—seductive, charming, deadly. On the other side, our master can be obedience. But surely this is a kind of shorthand. Our master can be not just any old obedience, but obedience to God. When we belong to obedience we again remember that we belong to Christ, who undid what Adam did by being perfectly obedient, and therefore perfectly free.

That is why Paul can say not only that we are slaves of obedience but also that we are slaves of righteousness. That is, we belong to the God who brings us into a right relationship with God's self through faith. The obedience of faith, we remember, is what Paul wants us all to pursue, receive, and enjoy. One imperfect way of talking about that is to say that we are faithful slaves to obedience and to righteousness.

In some ways here Paul expands on Jesus' words, words he may not himself have known: "No one can serve two masters; for a slave will either hate the one and love the other, or be devoted to the one and despise the other. You cannot serve God and wealth" (Matt. 6:24). Nor, says Paul, can you serve any of God's other great competitors—success, lust, power. All of them compete with God's mastery. Such competition is a good working definition of sin.

Do This!

Then Paul falls into the pattern that seems both so odd and inescapable: Remember who you belong to; now act like it.

> For just as you once presented your members as slaves to impurity and to greater and greater iniquity, so now present your members as slaves to righteousness for sanctification. (Rom. 6:19b–c)

When we read this sentence, it is hard not to believe that Paul is writing of sinfulness as displayed in selfish sexuality—and certainly there are enough clues in Romans 1 to help us think this may be part of it. But what Paul mainly reminds us of is that we are bodies, and what we do with our bodies is what *we* do. (*Our Bodies, Ourselves* is a book written to help women toward self-understanding, and Paul would think the title was right on target.) Our members, after all, include our tongues and our brains and our stomachs as well as our procreative organs. We can serve sin by gossip and overweening pride and gluttony as much as by promiscuity. For Paul sin is not primarily all those things that we do to induce anger in others and guilt in ourselves. Sin is that great, tyrannical, overweening master that takes control of us and drives us to do the very things we hate. The Hitler of our hearts.

As Christians we are part of the resistance, the underground, serving another Lord who demands other loyalties. We constantly seek to sabotage the power of sin by using tongues to praise God and encourage others; brains to rejoice in the divine wisdom; stomachs in moderation lest my banquet be another's famine; and sexuality in fidelity, responsibility, and joy.

Paul calls us to serve the right master by our right obedience. We present our members to righteousness—God's rightness—for sanctification. Sanctification just means "holiness." Remember Romans 1:7, where Paul addresses the Christians in Rome as "called to be saints," sanctified. Being sanctified is not some next step after having a right relationship to God. Being sanctified is the way righteousness clothes itself in the world. Sanctification is the hands and feet of righteousness, the obedience of faith. Saintliness and sanctification for Paul are not the property of a small subgroup of super Christians. When we are baptized we become saints, sanctified. Then, of course, comes the gift of living out our calling.

Wages and Gifts

Now this complicated theme gets more complicated and more clear. There are some masters who enslave their slaves, and there are some masters for whom service is perfect freedom. Those masters who enslave give out wages, tit for tat; you work for me, and I'll pay you. Because you need my approval to get your paycheck, you'll work harder and harder, and in the end you will not get a fat old bankroll but will simply work yourself to death. Sin works us to death.

To take an example from our own time, have you noticed how hard the tobacco industry has to work at its death-dealing subservience? The industry employs highly paid lobbyists and pseudo-scientists. It pays for ads enticing younger and younger people to take up the habit their elders are beginning to let go. It establishes international networks to sell abroad the stuff that is not selling as well at home as it used to. The enterprise is frantic. Corporations deal biological death to stave off economic death. Every paycheck has a price tag. Sin will do that to you, wear you out in its service and then send you out to die.

Paul says that if you go chasing sin you will get paid in the end. You will get what you work for, and what you are working for is death. On the other hand, if you receive grace, God's gift—sheer gift, free gift—you don't get death, you get life. You get eternal life—life worth living now and life with God beyond the now and then. This gift turns out not to be slavery after all. The gift is rather the son coming home from the far country saying: "Father, I have sinned against heaven and before you; I am no longer worthy to be called your son." And before he can get out the last line of the prepared speech—"Treat me like one of your hired hands"—the father shouts the gospel: "Quickly, bring out a robe—the best one—and put it on him; put a ring on his finger and sandals on his feet. And get the fatted calf and kill it, and let us eat and celebrate; for this son of mine was dead and is alive again" (Luke 15:21–24).

The gift is life, and that can only be a gift because it cannot be earned. Sin deals in wages; God deals in gifts. Sin is a tyrannical master; God's mastery is always moving us toward freedom and toward life.

God moves us toward "eternal life in Christ Jesus our Lord." Jesus does more than tell the story of the prodigal son coming home and the father running to meet him. Like the father, Jesus runs out to meet us. He has run to meet us before we ever turned to him.

Our preaching and teaching and conversation would be so different if we spent less time telling people to shape up and get better. We could spend more time reminding people how much goodness is given us in the grace of God. We are citizens of no mean country—God's realm. We belong to no mean family—the family of God. We are graced with no mean gifts—the gifts that God has given us in Jesus Christ. We can be the kind of people we are and stop pretending to be the backbiting grouches we acted like when we got up this morning.

Is the Law Itself Sinful? (Romans 7:1–25)

7:1 **Do you not know, brothers and sisters—for I am speaking to those who know the law—that the law is binding on a person only during that person's** lifetime? [2] Thus a married woman is bound by the law to her husband as long as he lives; but if her husband dies, she is discharged from the law concerning the husband. [3] Accordingly, she will be called an adulteress if she lives with another man while her husband is alive. But if her husband dies, she is free from that law, and if she marries another man, she is not an adulteress.

[4] In the same way, my friends, you have died to the law through the body of Christ, so that you may belong to another, to him who has been raised from the dead in order that we may bear fruit for God. [5] While we are living in the flesh, our sinful passions, aroused by the law, were at work in our members to bear fruit for death. [6] But now we are discharged from the law, dead to that which held us captive, so that we are slaves not under the old written code but in the new life of the Spirit.

[7] What then should we say? That the law is sin? By no means! Yet, if it had not been for the law, I would not have known sin. I would not have known what it is to covet if the law had not said: "You shall not covet." [8] But sin, seizing an opportunity in the commandment, produced in me all kinds of covetousness. Apart from the law sin lies dead. [9] I was once alive apart from the law, but when the commandment came, sin revived [10] and I died, and the very commandment that promised life proved to be death to me. [11] For sin, seizing an opportunity in the commandment, deceived me and through it killed me. [12] So the law is holy, and the commandment is holy and just and good.

[13] Did what is good, then, bring death to me? By no means! It was sin, working death in me through what is good, in order that sin might be shown to be sin, and through the commandment might become sinful beyond measure.

[14] For we know that the law is spiritual; but I am of the flesh, sold into slavery under sin. [15] I do not understand my own actions. For I do not do what I want, but I do the very thing I hate. [16] Now if I do what I do not want, I agree that the law is good. [17] But in fact it is no longer I that do it, but sin that dwells within me. [18] For I know that nothing good dwells within me, that is, in my flesh. I can will what is right, but I cannot do it. [19] For I do not do the good I want, but the evil I do not want is what I do. [20] Now if I do what I do not want, it is no longer I that do it, but sin that dwells within me.

[21] So I find it to be a law that when I want to do what is good, evil lies close at hand. [22] For I delight in the law of God in my inmost self, [23] but I see in my members another law at war with the law of my mind, making me captive to the law of sin that dwells in my members. [24] Wretched man that I am! Who will rescue me from this body of death? [25] Thanks be to God through Jesus Christ our Lord!

So then, with my mind I am a slave to the law of God, but with my flesh I am a slave to the law of sin.

Dead to the Law, Alive to Christ (Romans 7:1–6)

Paul's illustration or parable is either complicated or confused. Yet we can understand the claim he is making. He begins by drawing an illustration from the law, which would work equally well for both the Gentiles and the Jews in his audience. The marriage law is binding on a woman only while her husband is alive. The death of the husband liberates her from the power of that law to define her. Clearly Paul wants to insist that Christians have died to the power of the law. However, in this illustration it is not quite clear whether it is Christ's death or the "death" of Christians in baptism that makes the difference. The issue is further complicated by the fact that in the words "in the same way" Paul compares both Christians and Christ to the living parties who survived the death of the imaginary husband. In this part of the illustration it is not that someone has died under the law, but that the law itself has died or at least lost is binding power.

If we back away from the illustration to the argument, the point is fairly clear. We remember that Paul thinks in terms of the great shift of the ages, from the old age when sin and the law reigned supreme and claimed our allegiance to the new age when Christ reigns supreme and claims our allegiance through faith.

We are defined by whom we belong to. In the old age we might appropriately have belonged to the power of the law. But the power of the law, like the power of sin, has been defeated in the cross of Jesus Christ. Now we belong, not to the law, but to Christ who defeated the law, or completed the law, or finished the law by his death.

> But now we are discharged from the law, dead to that which held us captive, so that we are slaves not under the old written code but in the new life of the Spirit. (Rom. 7:6)

This verse sums up the illustration and also points us ahead to the claim of Romans 8:2, "For the law of the Spirit of life in Christ Jesus has set you free from the law of sin and of death." As Christians we live in submission to Jesus Christ, but as Christians we also live in the freedom of God's Spirit, which is precisely the sign of that life-giving submission.

Is the Law Sin? (Romans 7:7–25)

Paul's claim that the law is a mark of the old age, the age in which we sin and disobey, could easily lead to the assumption that the law itself is sin, or sinful. The Roman Christians might think that the law is itself disaster and not gift. Paul will go to great length in Romans 9—11 to insist on the fact that the law is blessing, but he begins here to build his case as he makes two claims:

1. Like sin, law belongs to the old age which for Christians ends in the cross and resurrection of Jesus Christ.
2. Unlike sin, the law is not a violation of God's purpose but part of God's purpose—even though it may work to increase sin.

Two features of these verses help us understand Paul's somewhat complicated argument.

First, the "I" to whom Paul refers is not really the autobiographical "I." We don't know much about Paul's sense of his own sinfulness before he was called to be an apostle, although Philippians 3 suggests that he was rather more proud of his accomplishments than ashamed of his sins. In any case, the "I" here is a way of talking about all of us, humankind, as we find ourselves apart from God's making us right in Jesus Christ. We remember that Paul's great claim is that all of us are made righteous through faith because all of us have sinned and fallen short of the glory of God. These verses describe that "I" who is "all of us."

Second, not very far in the background of Paul's thinking is the story of Adam and Eve in the garden. We have already seen (Rom. 5:12–21) that, for Paul, Adam is the great representative of what it means to be human apart from Jesus Christ. What we get in Romans 7:7–12 is in part an interpretation of the story of the Garden of Eden so that we can see ourselves described there. Adam and Eve's story is our story, and in this chapter at least, the "I" to which Paul refers is the "I" who lives out Adam's story.

Rather than give a verse-by-verse discussion of this text, let me try to show how Paul reads Adam's story as our story. When Adam was in the garden, in the very beginning, there was no law, no commandment. Then God gave him one commandment: You shall not eat of the fruit of the tree of good and evil (Gen. 2:17). Now the commandment was a good commandment, but it gave opportunity to sin which wouldn't have been aroused apart from the commandment. If God hadn't said don't eat of the one tree, Adam and Even might never have thought of eating of that tree. (The serpent doesn't play a role in Paul's rethinking of the story.) But when God said don't touch that fruit, Adam and Even began to covet the one thing in the garden that had not been given them, the one thing reserved for God alone.

Mark Twain wonderfully catches this aspect of the story from Genesis: "Adam was but human—this explains it all. He did not want the apple for the apple's sake, he wanted it only because it was forbidden" (*Pudd'nhead Wilson*, at head of chapter 2).

So the law served sin in two ways. First, it enticed Adam and Eve to think about disobedience, as they wouldn't have thought of disobedience on their own. Second, it made the sin all the worse, because not only did they do the wrong thing, they did the wrong thing in explicit violation of what God told them.

In both these ways it may help to think of rearing children. Everyone who has been around children knows that one way to entice, if not to guarantee, a particular behavior is to forbid it explicitly: "Whatever you do, don't raid the cookie jar." "Cookie jar? Oh, boy! I hadn't even thought of that."

Everyone who has tried to discipline children knows that an offense seems more offensive if it takes place in explicit violation of a direct instruction. If the children happen upon the cookies we were saving for company and eat them up, that's unfortunate, but we aren't too angry. If the children head for the cookie jar just after we've said no, righteous indignation comes more easily, if not more appropriately.

Then in Romans 7:13–25 Paul draws another analogy (comparison), not so much from the history of Adam and Eve as from the experience we have all had, apart from Christ, when we want to do one thing and yet end up doing another. The fact that we want to do what is right shows that what is right *is* right. The fact that we don't do what we want to do shows that there is something even stronger than our principles. That something, says Paul, is sin. Remember, for Paul sin is a great and tyrannical power that can almost force us into obedience.

The inner self that wants to do the good proves that the law (which I long to obey) is itself good. The "members"—tongue, brain, hands, feet—which refuse to attend my own good intentions, show that sin is strong, seductive, sneaky.

Remember that when Jesus deals with evil in the Gospels, he often casts out demons. We don't often think that way about evil, but for Paul sin is like a demon, because sin is a power we can't control and from which we cannot free ourselves. As Jesus casts out demons by the power of God, so God's power alone can free us from sin.

"Wretched man that I am!" cries Paul. "Who will rescue me from this body of death?" That is, Who will deliver me from the body that shows allegiance to sin and therefore marches me straight toward death? Paul concludes by describing his dilemma, a dilemma that shows that the law and sin are closely related but are by no means the same: "So then, with my mind I am a slave to the law of God, but with my flesh I am a slave to the law of sin." But the law of sin is not God's law, not Torah, not what Adam disobeyed and Moses later commanded.

Paul's problem, it seems quite clear, is not really the problem of the apostle Paul anymore. Paul does not wake up each morning, look in the mirror, and say: "Wretched man that I am! Who will rescue me from this body of death?" This is Paul as Adam's man looking ahead to Paul as Christ's man. This is Paul thinking about life before the cross turned everything around.

Even before this statement of the dilemma, after the cry of wretchedness (where Paul means all of us apart from Christ), Paul gives us a clue to the gospel with which he began and to which he will return: "Thanks be to God through Jesus Christ our Lord!" (v. 25).

Some interpreters think that line belongs somewhere else in the letter, say just before chapter 8. However, I think this sentence shows us that Paul always understands law and sin in the light of the good news that in Jesus Christ we have a great deal to be thankful for. Paul gives thanks to the one God who through the Son provides righteousness, life, freedom.

There is an ongoing debate among students of Romans 7:7–25. When Paul refers to his wretchedness as a sinful person, does he refer to his life as a Christian or to life before one knows Christ? Our discussion clearly suggests that Paul is referring to our life in Adam, our life before faith and baptism. Martin Luther read Romans as the basis for his claim that the Christian person is *simul justus et peccator*, at the same time justified and a sinner. Paul, however, believes that each of us was once *peccator* but is now *justus*.

> I once was lost, but now am found,
> Was blind, but now I see.

It is entirely possible that we will decide that Luther's reading of Romans as a description of the ongoing Christian dilemma describes our lives beautifully (see his *Lectures on Romans*). If we decide that, we will be deciding for Luther's imaginative reading of Paul's rather different claim that we are now no longer under sin, but under righteousness.

LIFE IN THE SPIRIT, LIFE IN CHRIST
Romans 8:1–39

Romans 8 is the magnificent response to the issues raised in Romans 6 and 7, to the whole argument that begins with Romans 5, and, in many ways, to the presentation of Paul's gospel from Romans 1:1 on. One could argue that Romans 8 is the central chapter for the whole epistle. Everything in chapters 1—7 leads up to it, and everything in chapters 9—16 grows out of it. For purposes of study the chapter can be divided into four parts: vv. 1–11, 12–17, 18–30, and 31–39.

The Spirit of Life (Romans 8:1–11)

8:1 **There is therefore now no condemnation for those who are in Christ Jesus. 2 For the law of the Spirit of life in Christ Jesus has set you free from the law of sin and of death. 3 For God has done what the law, weakened by the flesh, could not do: by sending his own Son in the likeness of sinful flesh, and to deal with sin, he condemned sin in the flesh, 4 so that the just requirement of the law might be fulfilled in us, who walk not according to the flesh but according to the Spirit. 5 For those who live according to the flesh set their minds on the things of the flesh, but those who live according to the Spirit set their minds on the things of the Spirit. 6 To set the mind on the flesh is death, but to set the mind on the Spirit is life and peace. 7 For this reason the mind that is set on the flesh is hostile to God; it does not submit to God's law—indeed it cannot, 8 and those who are in the flesh cannot please God.**

9 But you are not in the flesh; you are in the Spirit, since the Spirit of God dwells in you. Anyone who does not have the Spirit of Christ does not belong to him. 10 But if Christ is in you, though the body is dead because of sin, the Spirit is life because of righteousness. 11 If the Spirit of him who raised Jesus from the dead dwells in you, he who raised Christ from the dead will give life to your mortal bodies also through his Spirit that dwells in you.

Here is good news again, sheer gospel. There is therefore—because of everything Paul has told us—no condemnation for those who are in Christ Jesus. The law, which condemned those like Adam, who coveted what was not theirs, does not condemn those in Christ. The conscience, which condemned those Gentiles who fell into idolatry, does not condemn those in Christ. Those in Christ do not live under either the law of Moses or the law written on our hearts: we live under a different reality entirely—the reality of God's own Spirit.

The NRSV has chosen to use a capital letter with "Spirit" each time the word appears in this section. That seems an appropriate acknowledgment of the fact that for Paul the Spirit is closely related to the living Christ, the Lord of the church and of creation. While Paul does not develop any full-fledged doctrine of the Trinity, the Spirit is certainly God's presence among the faithful.

In order to understand verses 1–11 we need to remember that Paul believes that in Jesus Christ a great shift has taken place in human history and in the history of each believer. The old age of the flesh has passed away and the new age of the Spirit has come. Recall that at the very beginning of the epistle, Paul writes that Christ was designated Son of God by the Spirit at his resurrection (Rom. 1:4). The Spirit is the gift of God in the new age brought about by Christ's dying and rising again.

It may be that Paul has in mind the verse from Joel that is so central to the story of Pentecost in Acts 2: "Then afterward I will pour out my spirit on all flesh" (Joel 2:28). Acts interprets "afterward" somewhat differently: "In the last days . . . I will pour out my Spirit upon all flesh" (Acts 2:17). Certainly, for Paul the day of Jesus Christ is the last days, or the first days of the new creation.

Paul wants to emphasize the shift from the old age to the new for several reasons. First, he wishes to underline what he has been suggesting in chapters 6 and 7. Christians no longer belong to the old age of sin and death but to the new law of obedience and life. We live with Christ, not with Adam, and we need to know who we are.

Second, Paul wants to remind the Romans that they do not live under the law, the Torah. The Torah, for all its blessedness, was a blessing for the old age, not for the new. It has no place in the new age because it did not finally bring righteousness. In the old age, when people lived in the flesh, they were disobedient, even though they had the law. In the new age, people can be obedient because they have the Spirit. It is God's Spirit that makes possible the obedience of faith. The obedience of faith is not our accomplishment. It is not our discovery of some new and better law. It is an entirely different way of living: living in the Spirit.

The third reason that it is so important for Paul that Christians now live in the Spirit is that the Spirit is God's gift to all who have faith through Jesus Christ. The law was a gift to the Jews, but God is not the God of the Jews only, so the law cannot be God's blessing for this new age where Jew and Gentile come together.

Paul's fourth reason is that the Spirit is a gift not only because it opens a right relationship to God through our faithful obedience but because it is the promise of eternal life. The Spirit provides obedient life now; life with God for eternity. The Spirit gives us a taste of what eternal life will be. In the Spirit God dwells with us, as in eternity we shall dwell with God. In 1 Corinthians 13:12 Paul writes: "Now I know only in part; then I will know fully, even as I have been fully known." The Holy Spirit is the gift by which we know God in part, and we know that we are already fully known. The Holy Spirit is God's promise that one day we will also fully know.

Here, in Romans 8:1–11, Paul reminds the Roman Christians that they no longer walk according to the flesh. It is easy for us to think that Paul is primarily concerned about what we call the "sins of the flesh"—hurtful sexuality, habitual misuse of substances, gluttony. Paul would probably have something to say about each of these abuses, but life in the flesh for him is primarily life in the old age. Life in the flesh is the life of bondage to sin. To be in the flesh is to belong to the old powers of sin, which keep us self-centered, obsessively worried about our own worthiness, or obsessively interested in proving that we don't need to live up to any standards. To be in the flesh is to belong to the old powers of the law, which seemed to Paul to keep us running after something we would never achieve: our own righteousness. Life in the flesh is the life that brags about me: how good I am, or how liberated from ordinary principles, or how pious. Life in the flesh is life that worries about me: Am I getting enough? Am I giving enough? Am I pious enough? or impious enough?

To be in the Spirit is to belong to God in Jesus Christ, who brings us into a right relationship with God's self as a free gift. To be in the Spirit is to be bound to the one master who gives us freedom.

Think again of the parable of the prodigal son. Both brothers live in the age of the flesh. The young brother is in bondage to sin: Let's see how free I can be. The older brother is in bondage to law: Look how upright I am. The father invites them to a new age of the Spirit, that banquet where all of us are God's children, recipients of good gifts we could not earn, and bound to one another because we are offspring of the same loving parent.

So, too, Romans 8:1–11 is an invitation to us today to find our meaning not in the achievements that divide us from one another but in the grace that unites us. Barriers of denomination, doctrine, practice, and piety give way before the gift we all share: the Spirit God gives us through Jesus Christ our Lord.

Life in the Spirit (Romans 8:12–17)

8:12 **So then, brothers and sisters, we are debtors, not to the flesh, to live according to the flesh—** [13] **for if you live according to the flesh, you will die; but if by the Spirit you put to death the deeds of the body, you will live.** [14] **For all who are led by the Spirit of God are children of God.** [15] **For you did not receive a spirit of slavery to fall back into fear, but you have received a spirit of adoption. When we cry, "Abba! Father!"** [16] **it is that very Spirit**

bearing witness with our spirit that we are children of God, [17] and if children, then heirs, heirs of God and joint heirs with Christ—if, in fact, we suffer with him so that we may also be glorified with him.

Paul now provides the evidence that the Roman churches belong to God's Spirit. The evidence is that in their worship they cry out "Abba!" which is Aramaic for father. Surely the only reason they can call God "Father" is that they are God's children. They are children adopted to join the family of Jesus Christ, who is God's Son from the beginning.

Perhaps the Romans cried out "Abba" as part of their worship, a kind of affirmation, as we might sing the Doxology or the Gloria Patri, or (also using a foreign language) say "alleluia!" Perhaps the Romans prayed "Abba" when they began the Lord's Prayer: "Abba, Father in heaven . . ." If so, then we are joined to the first Roman Christians by our own worship, since we too pray week after week the "Our Father." The fact that we pray "Our Father" proves that we, too, are God's adopted sons and daughters. We are united to Jesus Christ, who is God's Son from the beginning. We are united to all other faithful people who also pray that prayer and are also, therefore, God's sons and daughters. We are united to the Roman Christians and to the communion of saints through all ages who have prayed that prayer. And, whether we think of it this way or not, we live in the Spirit, which unites us to one another and to Christ.

What if an ecumenical discussion of our common faith began with the Lord's Prayer before talking about the creeds or church organization? What do we all pray together? What does that prayer tell us about our relationship to one another and to Christ? One day surely we will all be able to come together at the Lord's Table, as Paul wanted Roman Christians to come together. But as we wait for that, surely it is the gift of the Spirit that we can pray together, using the same words: "Our Father . . ." Surely when we say "*Our* Father" we cannot possibly mean "Father of us Presbyterians" or "Father of us Catholics." The Spirit inspires us to say a prayer that includes all faithful people. When we pray as Christians, it's not just who we pray for that matters, it's who we pray with—our brothers and sisters in the Spirit, all of them.

What becomes even more evident in these verses is that the Spirit is not somehow an extra god separate from God the Creator or from Jesus Christ the Son. The Spirit of God is what binds us to Jesus Christ. For Paul the Spirit is Christ's Spirit, almost, one could say, Christ with us.

The last half-verse of the section provides a transition to the discussion of suffering and the hope that follows suffering. Hope is also a sign and gift of the Spirit "if, in fact, we suffer with him so that we may also be glorified with him."

The Spirit, Suffering, and Hope (Romans 8:18–30)

8:18 I consider that the sufferings of this present time are not worth comparing with the glory about to be revealed to us. [19] For the creation waits with eager longing for the revealing of the children of God; [20] for the creation was subjected to futility, not of its own will but by the will of the one who subjected it, in hope [21] that the creation itself will be set free from its bondage to decay and will obtain the freedom of the glory of the children of God. [22] We know that the whole creation has been groaning in labor pains until now; [23] and not only the creation, but we ourselves, who have the first fruits of the Spirit, groan inwardly while we wait for adoption, the redemption of our bodies. [24] For in hope we were saved. Now hope that is seen is not hope. For who hopes for what is seen? [25] But if we hope for what we do not see, we wait for it with patience.

[26] Likewise the Spirit helps us in our weakness; for we do not know how to pray as we ought, but that very Spirit intercedes with sighs too deep for words. [27] And God, who searches the heart, knows what is the mind of the Spirit, because the Spirit intercedes for the saints according to the will of God.

[28] We know that all things work together for good for those who love God, who are called according to his purpose. [29] For those whom he foreknew he also predestined to be conformed to the image of his Son, in order that he might be the firstborn within a large family. [30] And those whom he predestined he also called; and those whom he called he also justified; and those whom he justified he also glorified.

Here the contrast between the age of the flesh and the age of the Spirit is expanded and enriched. When we receive the gift of the Spirit, we receive the first taste of that glory which enters history in the cross and resurrection of Jesus Christ but whose splendor is yet to come in its fullness.

Even though we know the Spirit, Paul reminds us that we live under the ongoing conditions of the age of the flesh, which is defeated but not destroyed. The sign of the power of sin is that faithful people still suffer, but the promise of the Spirit is that suffering will give way to our full fellowship in God's own family.

Only here in all of the New Testament do we hear of a hope that finds its expression often in Jewish writing. Our hope is not only for the redemption of human beings but for the redemption of the whole creation (8:18–22). Here Paul implies that Adam's disobedience not only plunged humankind into the certainty of death but plunged all creation into decay.

God's will is not just for restored people but for a restored universe. We do not see that universe yet, but we live in hope. We have hope, and we have a promise to hope for.

So, too, if Paul's great claim is that there is one God both for Jews and Gentiles, then surely this is the one God who is God of all creation and whose providential care cannot exclude any part of what God has created. We remember Abraham, who had faith in God's promise that out of barrenness life would come. Now we are called to have faith in God's promise that out of suffering glory will come.

In an age when we suffer from our refusal to see our relationship to the rest of God's creation, we may be especially chastened and strengthened by the reminder that the glory toward which we move includes humankind and the whole nonhuman world as well. No one can describe what that means; it pushes us toward poetry, as it did Gerard Manley Hopkins, who saw the promise, the loss, and the hope of the Holy Spirit:

> The world is charged with the grandeur of God.
>   It will flame out, like shining from shook foil;
>   It gathers to a greatness, like the ooze of oil
> Crushed. Why do men then now not reck his rod?
> Generations have trod, have trod, have trod;
>   And all is seared with trade; bleared, smeared with toil;
>   And wears man's smudge and shares man's smell: the soil
> Is bare now, nor can foot feel, being shod.
>
> And for all this, nature is never spent;
>   There lives the dearest freshness deep down things;
> And though the last lights off the black West went
>   Oh, morning, at the brown brink eastward, springs—
> Because the Holy Ghost over the bent
>   World broods with warm breast and with ah! bright wings.

In Romans 8:26–27 Paul again looks to our worship to show the evidence of God's Spirit. As our praying "Abba" proves that the Spirit makes us God's children, the fact that our inarticulate praying nonetheless is heard and blessed by God shows that God's Spirit is present with us, to plead for us or intercede for us. We don't know whether Paul has a specific practice in mind here, like speaking in tongues in worship. Whether we speak in tongues or only know that our best prayers are inadequate to our hearts' longing, we are comforted to know that God's Spirit prays with us—for us.

This claim that the Spirit intercedes for us ties directly to the larger claims of Romans 8:28–30. Our prayers to God really begin with God and end with God. Our lives begin with God and end with God. When Paul says that we are predestined to be conformed to the image of God's son, he reminds us that all is grace: our being and our becoming and our ending. Whether or not that means that God foreknows and even plans each word we speak or write, each deed we do, each love we share, Paul never says. What he does say is that God is God, and our lives are in God's hands from birth to death and beyond death. Of course God shapes our lives to a particular purpose: that we should be conformed to Jesus Christ. Again the picture is that of a family into which we are adopted: calling Jesus "Lord" and God "Abba," Father.

It is within this strong faith—the faith that God shapes us toward our life with Christ—that Paul makes the claim we find in Romans 8:28. Different translations of the text come from use of slightly different Greek manuscripts.

The NRSV translates the text in this way: "We know that all things work together for good for those who love God, who are called according to his purpose." Most ancient texts support this reading.

Several ancient manuscripts, however, including the oldest, a text called papyrus 46, have a slightly different Greek sentence that the Revised Standard Version used in its translation: "We know that in everything God works for good with those who love him, who are called according to his purpose." This reading reminds us that Paul is not saying that for Christians everything is always for the best. He is saying that in everything God works *toward* the best in partnership with those who love God.

I have found that to be a comforting reading of the text when I have grieved or shared with others in their grief. Christians do not need to say that every tragedy or loss is part of God's plan. We can say that in every tragedy or loss God is still God and still moves our lives and all of history toward what is good.

Even when contemplating the enormous tragedies of human history, natural disaster, or human viciousness, faith reminds us that God is still at work in the midst of evil, working toward the good. The question, Why did God let this happen? is unanswerable. The questions we may begin to answer are, What can God do with this evil to help bring about the good? How can we be God's partners, God's servants in that work?

Though the RSV reading makes this claim explicit, both the RSV and the NRSV surely show that what Paul believes is not that everything turns out all right every minute, but that God has destined good for faithful people and for the whole creation. In the RSV reading, at least, God works with us toward that good.

If God Is for Us (Romans 8:31–39)

8:31 **What then are we to say about these things? If God is for us, who is against us?** [32] **He who did not withhold his own Son, but gave him up for all of us, will he not with him also give us everything else?** [33] **Who will bring any charge against God's elect? It is God who justifies.** [34] **Who is to condemn? It is Christ Jesus, who died, yes, who was raised, who is at the right hand of God, who indeed intercedes for us.** [35] **Who will separate us from the love of Christ? Will hardship, or distress, or persecution, or famine, or nakedness, or peril, or sword?** [36] **As it is written,**
> **"For your sake we are being killed all day long;**
>   **we are accounted as sheep to be slaughtered."**
[37]**No, in all these things we are more than conquerors through him who loved us.** [38]**For I am convinced that neither death, nor life, nor angels, nor rulers, nor things present, nor things to come, nor powers,** [39] **nor height, nor depth, nor anything else in all creation, will be able to separate us from the love of God in Christ Jesus our Lord.**

This whole passage is a ringing affirmation of God's goodness to us in Jesus Christ—against all the forces that can be arrayed in opposition to us. As is so often the case in Romans, Paul emphasizes both what God has already done for us in Jesus Christ, what Christ does for us now, and what we can *hope* for in the light of Christ's love.

What God Has Done for Us in Jesus Christ

God has given us his own son. There are echoes here of Genesis 22, in which Abraham is asked to give his son, and for the Christian reader there are certainly recollections of John 3:16, a passage that Paul did not know but whose themes fit his own concerns. For Paul the gift of Jesus Christ crucified is not only an example of God's love: it is the act of God's love. It is God doing love among us and for the whole creation. God has also raised Jesus from the dead. This is the foreshadowing of God's great victory to which the whole passage will point.

What Jesus Christ Does For Us Now

Because Christ is risen from the dead, we can count on his intercession for us with God. Taken literally, this seems to mean that Christ is with

God pleading to God on our behalf. Even if we take Paul's promise less literally, we can affirm with Paul that Jesus Christ is God's goodwill on our behalf, and the resurrection is the guarantee that the love of God for us in Christ cannot be conquered by death but continues to stir God's heart even now. This is not true just because God remembers Jesus kindly but because Jesus is raised to eternal life, with God. For us.

What We Hope For

God has already given us the greatest gift imaginable, the gift of God's own son. Because of this we can count on a gift that is, strangely, less valuable than the invaluable gift of Christ, but still a promise of hope. We can count on "everything"! The gift of Christ is more than everything, but having received more than everything, we can count on everything, too.

Paul expands on this in two ways. First, he says, we are "more than conquerors" (v. 36). In the light of persecution and distress, we not only survive, we receive God's eternal glory. A pastor I know reminded me that for Paul we are also more than conquerors because we are *other* than conquerors. We shall see in Romans 13 that the Christian life for Paul is not the life of conquest but of loving compassion. Those who are more than conquerors are those who refuse to conquer. Those who refuse to seek victory are victorious. Those who do not glory in their own accomplishments can boast in the glory of the Lord, which will finally include the faithful, too.

Second, Paul reminds us that no power in creation can separate us from God's love in Jesus Christ. The list of the creation's powers—death, life, angels, heights, depths—reminds us that for Paul the world is populated with forces that call for our allegiance and threaten to control us. We could make our own list, but the point would be the same. We are driven and enticed by forces stronger than ourselves and weaker than God. The power that is greater than anything in creation is the power of the Creator. It is the love of the Creator that we know in Jesus Christ our Lord.

Paul is writing this letter to Christians who know persecution. Jewish Christians in Rome are just back from banishment. Whether the Roman Christians know it or not, Nero's own persecution is just around the corner, and Paul will end his own life a prisoner in Rome. Created powers assail the faithful on every side. Paul quotes Psalm 44:22: "Because of you we are being killed all day long, and accounted as sheep for the slaughter." Whether the Romans remember it or not, Paul surely knows the rest of the Psalm. It is a plea to God.

Rouse yourself! Why do you sleep, O LORD?
  Awake, do not cast us off forever!
Why do you hide your face?
  Why do you forget our affliction and oppression?
For we sink down to the dust;
  our bodies cling to the ground.
Rise up, come to our help.
  Redeem us for the sake of your steadfast love.
                              (Psalm 44:23–26)

For Paul, God has answered that plea in Jesus Christ. Christ is God's steadfast love in whom God reveals God's face and raises us from the dust to eternal glory.

It is essential for Paul that we acknowledge that it is *God* who has answered our plea for help. "It is God who justifies." It is God who makes righteous—that strong claim with which our epistle began. It is God who brings us into a right relationship with God's own self. Some versions of what God has done in Jesus Christ suggest that Jesus heroically persuaded God to change God's mind and, instead of punishing us, to redeem us. This is not Paul's faith. For Paul it is God who from the beginning intended to make us righteous and who does make us righteous, provides a right relationship in Jesus Christ. Christ is not our defense attorney and God the divine prosecutor in some cosmic court scene. Christ is God's plan for us, God's gift, God's intention, God's victory. Christ is not our victory over an angry God. Christ is God's victory over sin and death.

If the whole purpose of this letter so far has been to insist that there is one God, of Jew and Greek and of the whole creation, and that the one God seeks to bring the whole creation into a right relationship with God's self through the one man Jesus Christ, then here the letter reaches its climax. Here is the picture of a victory not yet realized but well under way. (Like D-day, which was not the end of World War II but the beginning of the end. Like the Montgomery bus boycott, which was not the end of legalized segregation in the United States but the beginning of the end.) In God's final victory, God will lay claim to the whole creation by the love God has shown in Jesus Christ. We will be more than conquerors because no force in heaven or on earth can separate us from that love, which is God's victory on our behalf. God's glory and our glory, too.

The passage is of course more rich and powerful than we can say. It is the ringing affirmation in which Christians have found their comfort from the first century to the threshold of the twenty-first. Of course to this day we may be regarded as sheep to be slaughtered, if not by persecution, then by the slings and arrows of our sometimes outrageous everyday existence. Yet the Christian does not sit down at the end of each day and tote up the column of blessings and disasters to see if God is God. The Christian looks at Good Friday and Easter, at the love of God in Jesus Christ, and knows that God is God and shall be God and that nothing will be able to separate us from God's love. That is our hope. That is our confidence.

4. God's Faithfulness
Romans 9—11

At first glance it looks as though Paul radically shifts the subject of his letter at the beginning of chapter 9. He has just made the powerful affirmation that nothing can separate the faithful from the love of God in Jesus Christ. Now he enters into a long discussion of the place of Israel in God's providential plan, which he begins by asserting in a prayer that *he* would be willing to be separated from the love of God if his separation would mean inclusion for his brothers and sisters.

Yet for at least two reasons the material in chapters 9—11 is an appropriate continuation of Paul's claims in Romans 5—8. For one thing, theologically, Paul needs to reaffirm his faith that God is just and that God fulfills God's promises. One reading of Israel's history might be that God has turned away from Israel in order to embrace the church. But such a reading would suggest to Paul that God's mind has changed about entering a right relationship with all people, and God's faithfulness is precisely at the heart of what Paul claims. God's mind does not change.

For another thing, we remember that Paul is deeply concerned from beginning to end in this letter to show the ways in which Jews and Gentiles alike come together as part of God's plan and also to show how Jewish Christians and Gentile Christians come together in the Roman churches. The larger discussion of Israel and the Gentiles has immediate practical application in the self-understanding and the practice of the Roman communities (as we shall see when we look at Romans 12—16).

Chapters 9—11 of Romans provide a clear look at Paul's understanding of God's sovereignty, that is, God's creative power, which rules over lives and over history.

Paul does not provide any systematic doctrine of predestination. (He is not worried about systems.) What we do see in these chapters is that his great concern is not for God's plan for each individual soul, although certainly we know from his own statements that God's plan for him and for each Christian is important. Instead, Paul's great concern is God's plan for history. Does history have a purpose, and, especially, does God keep promises to the people Israel, and then to other people as well? We also see here Paul's faith that God moves history toward God's purposes. God has known from the beginning that the goal of history is that all things should find their meaning and life in God.

What Paul does not address is the question whether God knows in advance or plans in advance the details of every human life. He never raises the question whether God knew that you would have cereal and toast for breakfast this morning or would doze off as you read this chapter this evening.

We do know that Paul always assumes that we as individuals have an important choice to make: Will we turn to Christ in the obedience of faith? It may be that God elected us from the beginning to be among the faithful. It is certainly true that faith is a gift. But it is equally true that we are called to *be* faithful.

Certain philosophical questions that worry us, like the relationship between predestination and free will, don't bother Paul at all. Paul's questions—and answers—are these:

1. Is God a God who keeps God's promises? (Yes.)
2. Are we called to accept those promises through faith? (Yes again.)

ELECTION BY GOD, REJECTION BY ISRAEL
Romans 9:1–29

Paul's Plea for Israel
(Romans 9:1–5)

9:1 **I am speaking the truth in Christ—I am not lying; my conscience confirms it by the Holy Spirit—** 2 **I have great sorrow and unceasing anguish in my heart.** 3 **For I could wish that I myself were accursed and cut off from Christ for the sake of my own people, my kindred according to the flesh.** 4 **They are Israelites, and to them belong the adoption, the glory, the covenants, the giving of the law, the worship, and the promises;** 5 **to them belong the patriarchs, and from them, according to the flesh, comes the Messiah, who is over all, God blessed forever. Amen.**

Throughout Romans, Paul draws on scripture, on what we call the Old Testament, to find the themes and the evidence for his claims. In chapters 9—11, his reliance on scripture is particularly clear. Of course, his whole purpose here is to understand God's plan for Israel in the light of what God has done for all of humankind in Jesus Christ. The place to discover the nature of God's plan for Israel is the scripture God has given to Israel as charter and guide.

Moreover, often in this section of Romans Paul implicitly compares himself to some of the great figures of Israel's past, showing a continuity in call and purpose between the prophets and himself. The first great figure to whom he compares himself is Moses, and the second is Elijah. (We have no evidence that Paul knew the story of Jesus' transfiguration, when Moses and Elijah appeared on the mountain to validate Jesus' ministry. For both Paul and the gospel tradition, Moses and Elijah represent the law and the prophets. They are at the heart of Israel's own tradition.)

The first implicit comparison—the comparison between Paul and Moses—comes in the section we are now studying. When Paul says that he could wish to be cut off for the sake of "my kindred according to the flesh," that is, the historical people Israel, he echoes words that Moses speaks when he intercedes for his people, after the incident of the golden calf:

> On the next day Moses said to the people, "You have sinned a great sin. But now I will go up to the LORD; perhaps I can make atonement for your sin." So Moses returned to the LORD and said: "Alas, this people has sinned a great sin; they have made for themselves gods of gold. But now, if you will only forgive their sin—but if not, blot me out of the book that you have written." (Exod. 32:30–32)

In the first chapter of Romans, Paul explicitly says that the primary sin of the Gentiles has been idolatry. Now, by his recalling the story of the golden calf, it may be that he also claims that Israel has fallen into idolatry. Idolatry is worship of a god who is not God. The God who is God is the God who justifies, makes right, all people through faith. To worship a god who justifies only *some* people through the Torah is to worship a god who is not God. Israel's idolatry is now not to worship gods in the form of beasts (as it was in the wilderness; as it still is for the Gentiles). Israel's idolatry is to worship a local god, a national god, as if God were not the God of all people and of all creation. Of course, no other Jew of Paul's time or ours would understand Jewish belief in that way, but this sense of Israel's "idolatry" forms part of Paul's understanding. He is the new Moses because he calls his people away from other gods to the one God, the God of Jesus Christ.

The fact that Paul compares himself indirectly to Moses in no way detracts from the power of the oath he pronounces on himself. Verses 1–5 provide evidence of the deep, abiding, and painful love Paul has for his fellow Jews. Paul affirms in Philippians 3:8 that "I regard everything as loss because of the surpassing value of knowing Christ Jesus my Lord. For his sake I have suffered the loss of all things, and I regard them as rubbish, in order that I may gain Christ." Here Paul affirms that he is willing to give up Christ, who is more than all, for the sake of his fellow Jews. Like Moses with Israel, Paul here appears in an almost priestly role, willing not only to sacrifice but to sacrifice himself for the sake of the people.

The term that the NRSV translates "my kindred" in Romans 9:3 is the same term Paul uses to describe various people he greets in Romans 16:7 and 11. So some of his kindred are presumably known to the Roman Christians, and a few of his kindred have become Christians. They are perhaps among those returning to Rome after the exile imposed by Claudius.

Verses 4–5 have provided a puzzle for Christians through the years. Does Paul say that Jesus Christ is God, over all, blessed forever? Or does he say that Jesus is the Messiah, the Christ—and then pause to bless the God who sent Jesus? The Greek text can be translated either way. The NRSV translation suggests that Jesus *is* God or at least represents God: "from [Israel], according to the flesh, comes the Messiah, who is over all, God blessed forever." The marginal note suggests the other alternatives. One alternative makes the identification between Jesus and God even stronger: "from Israel according to the flesh comes the Messiah, who is God over all, blessed forever." The other alternative does not make that identification: "from Israel according to the flesh comes the Messiah. May he who is God over all be blessed forever."

Because the Greek texts do not include any punctuation, each of these translations is possible. However, the close similarity between this verse and Romans 1:3–4, where Jesus is son of David according to the flesh and Son of God according to the Spirit, may suggest that for Paul the term "messiah," so closely related to David's kingship, is inadequate to the strong claim he wishes to make for Jesus. Jesus is not only the one who has come to make Israel right, as the messiah would do. Jesus is the one who has come to restore the whole creation to righteousness, and such restoration is the work of God's own self.

At the very least, the echo of the golden calf story suggests that Paul wants to remind us that all the gifts Israel received—the promises, the covenant, the patriarchs—lead up to the one immeasurable gift of Jesus.

He is the immeasurable gift because he is the one who reveals the one God—who is God of the patriarchs, to be sure, but also of all the nations.

God's Gracious Choice
(Romans 9:6–18)

9:6 It is not as though the word of God had failed. For not all Israelites truly belong to Israel, [7] and not all of Abraham's children are his true descendants; but "It is through Isaac that descendants shall be named for you." [8] This means that it is not the children of the flesh who are the children of God, but the children of the promise are counted as descendants. [9] For this is what the promise said, "About this time I will return and Sarah shall have a son." [10] Nor is that all; something similar happened to Rebecca when she had conceived children by one husband, our ancestor Isaac. [11] Even before they had been born or had done anything good or bad (so that God's purpose of election might continue, [12] not by works but by his call) she was told, "The elder shall serve the younger." [13] As it is written,

"I have loved Jacob,
but I have hated Esau."

[14] What then are we to say? Is there injustice on God's part? By no means! [15] For he says to Moses,

"I will have mercy on whom I have mercy,
and I will have compassion on whom I have compassion."

[16] So it depends not on human will or exertion, but on God who shows mercy. [17] For the scripture says to Pharaoh, "I have raised you up for the very purpose of showing my power in you, so that my name may be proclaimed in all the earth." [18] So then he has mercy on whomever he chooses, and he hardens the heart of whomever he chooses.

The claim that all of God's activity leads up to God's gift in Jesus Christ still leaves Paul with a theological and practical problem. What about Israel? What about the undeniable fact that it is Gentiles who are flocking to join the churches and not, for the most part, Paul's fellow Jews? What does this say about Israel? Even more important, what does this say about God?

The answer is profound, but it can perhaps be put simply. God chooses who will be God's chosen people. The right name for God's chosen people is "Israel," but "Israel" does not always mean the biological descendants of the Hebrew fathers and mothers. "Israel" means those whom God has chosen—sometimes Jews and sometimes not.

Paul doesn't argue a case. He recalls familiar biblical stories. He recalls the meaning of the biblical stories. The story of Abraham and Sarah has already proved to be central to Paul's thinking. Abraham is the great example of faith; his faith in God was counted, reckoned, as righteousness. What Abraham trusted, the center of his faith, was that God would keep God's promises. What the one God promised to Abraham was Abraham's son Isaac. Isaac is the one who will provide Abraham's true family (see Gen. 21:12, which Paul here quotes). Abraham didn't need Isaac in order to have a male heir. Physically, Ishmael was already Abraham's son. Of course, because we have read Romans 4, we remember that for Paul, Abraham's true family are not his family "after the flesh," his biological heirs, but his family in faith. Abraham's family are those whose faith is like Abraham's faith: faith in the God who keeps promises.

It may be a slight exaggeration to say that, for Paul, Abraham's flesh, his intercourse with Sarah, is almost an accidental feature of Isaac's birth. Isaac is the child of God's promise. Perhaps Paul echoes his claim in Romans 1:4 that God's own son is also a Son of promise, whose sonship is confirmed, not through genealogy, but through the Holy Spirit. We are Isaac's brothers and sisters, but above all we are Jesus' brothers and sisters.

The story of Jacob and Esau provides another way of remembering that it is God's choice that determines who is chosen: not "the flesh," not biology or ancestry or good works. Indeed, Paul says, Jacob was chosen before he was born, before he could possibly accomplish anything. Jacob and Esau after all were twins, and Esau the elder twin at that. Yet the Bible bears witness that it is Jacob who inherits and passes on the promise—by whatever trickery. The quotation from Genesis again makes the point powerfully, almost painfully: "I have loved Jacob, but I have hated Esau."

Now Paul wisely anticipates the objections his readers may have, objections that we still have when we think about the story of Isaac, and especially the story of Jacob, and ask whether God is not finally unjust to those like Ishmael and Esau who got there first, who surely have the right to equality, if not priority.

At first glance, it looks as though Paul simply asserts that God is bigger than we are and therefore as a kind of divine bully God can do whatever God chooses. Yet a closer look reveals that Paul is proclaiming not only God's power but also God's goodness. The emphasis throughout these verses is on God's ability to show *mercy* as God wills. To be sure, God is sovereign over history, even over those who appear to reject God—like Pharaoh. We remember that nothing will be able to separate us from the love of God. That is a promise fulfilled in Jesus Christ, but foreshadowed in all the history of God's dealing with humankind, and especially with Israel. Not even Pharaoh can thwart God's purposes. Indeed, what

Pharaoh thinks are the devices and desires of his own heart can be the instruments by which God does God's will.

We need to acknowledge that Paul makes a mighty leap in all of this section of his letter. Passages that we would think applicable to Israel Paul applies to Gentiles, whom God has chosen to be heirs of God's promise. Passages that seem to refer to Israel's enemies Paul now hints might apply to the Jews themselves. Like Pharaoh's heart, the hearts of many in Israel have been hardened. This is a harsh word, but not of course the last word. It is a word made possible by Paul's beliefs. All of scripture points to Christ and his church. Abraham is not just the father of Israel but the father of all who are faithful. The promise fulfilled in Isaac *cannot* be a promise for Jews alone or God would be a tribal god, not Lord of all creation. Of course Paul means just that; the promise is not for Jews alone. We sometimes misread Paul to think that he says the promise is not for Jews at all. But this is precisely what Paul refuses to say. Otherwise we might fail to honor Israel as heirs of the promise. We might fail to honor God who made the promise in the first place.

One can see in this whole passage a working out of the great claim of Romans 8:28: In all things God works toward the good with those who love God. Those who love God may include Israel, but not Israel alone. The good toward which God works is Israel's good, but not Israel's alone. What seems now to be disastrous (the hardening of Pharaoh's heart; the failure to have faith in Christ on the part of so many in Israel) may still be used by God to move toward a good we can only begin to envision. We can envision that good because we have seen the cross and resurrection of Jesus Christ.

We see throughout this passage that Paul's great concern is not for the destiny of the individual believer, though of course that is always part of his interest. His great concern is for the meaning and movement of human history. Can we trust the God who makes promises when so much of history is not only unpromising but disastrous?

Gentile Christians have often misread Paul to think that he gives us permission to boast of being superior to our Jewish neighbors, thinking that God had abandoned them and turned to us instead. At its worst, such boasting has turned into discrimination and persecution. At its very worst, such boasting brought us the horrors of the Holocaust. In the light of the Holocaust, Jews and Christians have looked at the history of this tawdry century now ending and wondered whether God has forgotten God's promises.

Paul knew there were no easy answers to the pressing questions of relationships between Jews and Christians. In our time, we Christians live with the reminder that the cross is at the heart of God, and that if God is God, even at the end of this century, the final word must be the promise:

> I will have mercy on whom I have mercy,
> and I will have compassion on whom I have compassion.
>
> (Rom. 9:15)

And that promise cannot be for Gentiles alone.

Judgment Moves toward Mercy (Romans 9:19–29)

9:19 You will say to me then, "Why then does he still find fault? For who can resist his will?" 20 But who indeed are you, a human being, to argue with God? Will what is molded say to the one who molds it, "Why have you made me like this?" 21 Has the potter no right over the clay, to make out of the same lump one object for special use and another object for ordinary use? 22 What if God, desiring to show his wrath and to make known his power, has endured with much patience the objects of wrath that are made for destruction; 23 and what if he has done so in order to make known the riches of his glory for the objects of mercy, which he has prepared beforehand for glory— 24 including us whom he has called, not from the Jews only but also from the Gentiles? 25 As indeed he says in Hosea,
"Those who were not my people I will call 'my people,'
and her who was not beloved I will call 'beloved.'"
26 "And in the very place where it was said to them, 'You are not my people,'
there they shall be called children of the living God."
27 And Isaiah cries out concerning Israel, "Though the number of the children of Israel were like the sand of the sea, only a remnant of them will be saved; 28 for the Lord will execute his sentence on the earth quickly and decisively." 29 And as Isaiah predicted,
"If the Lord of hosts had not left survivors to us,
we would have fared like Sodom
and been made like Gomorrah."

As he so often does, Paul uses an imaginary conversation partner to raise a serious question: "Look, if the question of who gets chosen is entirely a matter of God's decision and not our own, how can God possibly blame those who don't get chosen?" Paul answers by saying that when we question in that way we do not honor God as God, the one who shows forth both power and mercy. Biblical scholar Paul Achtemeier rightly reminds us that when we raise such questions we fall again into the most grievous sin: idolatry. We do not share the Gentile love of wooden idols or Israel's love of a kind of local god. We fall into the most pervasive human idolatry: our love of ourselves. (Achtemeier, *Romans,* 161.)

We remember God's awe-inspiring word to Job:

> Who is this that darkens counsel by words without knowledge?
> Gird up your loins like a man,
>   I will question you, and you shall declare to me.
> (Job 38:2–3)

Since God is God, God comes to us not as the one to be questioned but as the one who questions. Yet, at the same time, the God who questions us is not only a God of power but, as Paul insists time and again, a God of mercy. Paul elaborates on God's merciful power in three ways here.

First, he uses the image of the potter and the clay, which Jeremiah used somewhat differently in Jeremiah 18:6. This again is a way of reminding us of God's sovereignty. God is not only powerful, God is purposeful. The Creator creates with purpose, both the pots that will be kept and the pots that will be destroyed. The final purpose of creation, of course, is glory. Here a theme that has recurred so often through this epistle appears again. God's purpose is to move those whom God chooses toward glory, which we do not yet see but which is foreshadowed in Jesus Christ.

There is a clear note of judgment here. We sing the old hymn, "Have thine own way, Lord! Have thine own way! Thou art the Potter; I am the clay. Mold me and make me after thy will." Yet it is clear that in this context Paul is not affirming only the potter's power to mold and create. He also affirms the potter's power to smash and destroy. God is God, and cannot be sentimentalized to fit our own views of pleasantness. However, we also note that, while there is no doubt that God is our judge, the purpose of judgment is always mercy—to bring those God chooses to glory. Most important in the context of Romans, because the merciful God is the one God of all people, God chooses for glory people "not from the Jews only but also from the Gentiles." We can turn that around: God chose a people not only from the Gentiles, as we Christians might self-righteously assume, but also from the Jews. Yet note that for Paul it is still the inclusion of the Gentiles that is surprising. Any fool knew that God intended glory for the Jews.

Second, Paul makes explicit what has been implicit in his discussion of Isaac, Jacob, and Pharaoh. The claim is not only that God chooses to use individuals as God wills. More important, God uses whole peoples to bring about God's glory. The quotation from Hosea makes clear that God's sovereign purpose calls forth people to be God's own people. Remember that this is the God who creates something out of nothing, Isaac out of a promise, a people out of no people. Again Paul has made a leap in the light of his faith in what God has done in Jesus Christ. Hosea sees a new people made up of a penitent Israel. For Paul the no people who are a new people are the Gentile Christians or perhaps Jewish and Gentile Christians who are now a new community, called by grace and united by faith: "children of the living God."

Third, Paul begins to suggest a way in which God continues to deal mercifully with Israel. Although the heart of the proclamation is still God's sovereign power to do as God wills, it is clear that what God sometimes wills is to choose a "remnant" to represent all of God's people destined for glory. Is this what has happened to Israel in Paul's time as in Isaiah's time? Paul begins to hint at an answer.

Remember that in all this Paul does not necessarily start by puzzling about God's sovereignty and predestining will. Paul may start (as Rom. 9:1–3 would suggest) by worrying about people he loves and wondering why they have not come to accept God's work in Jesus Christ. He knows that he has not come to Christ through any particular merit of his own. Paul's faith is God's gift, and the God who gives this gift is sovereign. God makes choices. Paul has been chosen, not because he is good, but because God is God.

Our own understanding of God's choice won't include any claim that God likes some people better than others, least of all any claim that God likes us better than others. It is all too easy for Christians to move from saying "I'm so blessed" to saying "I'm so nice." Paul's reminder of God's sovereignty helps warn us against such claims.

ISRAEL'S REJECTION OF GOD'S CALL
Romans 9:30–10:21

The Law of Righteousness; the Righteousness of Faith
(Romans 9:30–10:4)

9:30 **What then are we to say? Gentiles, who did not strive for righteousness, have attained it, that is, righteousness through faith; 31 but Israel, who did strive for the righteousness that is based on the law, did not succeed in fulfilling that law. 32 Why not? Because they did not strive for it on the ba-**

sis of faith, but as if it were based on works. They have stumbled over the stumbling stone, [33] as it is written,
"See, I am laying in Zion a stone that will make people stumble, a rock that will make them fall,
and whoever believes in him will not be put to shame."
10:1 Brothers and sisters, my heart's desire and prayer to God for them is that they may be saved. [2] I can testify that they have a zeal for God, but it is not enlightened. [3] For, being ignorant of the righteousness that comes from God, and seeking to establish their own, they have not submitted to God's righteousness. [4] For Christ is the end of the law so that there may be righteousness for everyone who believes.

We can best understand, or puzzle about, this passage if we begin with the last verse. The word that the NRSV translates "end" is the Greek word *telos*. As with our word "end," *telos* can have two meanings. It can mean the finish, conclusion: "I'm going home at the end of the movie." It can mean a goal, purpose: "To what end did she make that argument?"

In a similar way Paul may be saying either of two things. He may be saying that with Christ the law, the Torah, comes to an end; it's over. Or he can be saying that Christ is the goal to which Torah has pointed. The law finds its fulfillment in him. (This is what Jesus himself says in Matthew's Gospel: "Do not think that I have come to abolish the law or the prophets; I have come not to abolish but to fulfill" [Matt. 5:17].)

We cannot decide which of these claims Paul means by looking at this sentence alone. We really need to look at the whole of Romans.

On the one hand, everything we have seen in Romans suggests that the Old Testament does point to Jesus. Time and time again Paul quotes passages to show that God's plan from the beginning, the plan revealed in Torah, has been to make right the world in the gift of Jesus Christ. In that sense, Christ is the goal of the law.

On the other hand, it is clear, especially in these verses, that the law could not do what Christ has done. The law, the Torah, could not bring us into a right relationship with God. Paul has different ways of describing the law's inadequacy in different sections of Romans—but what he makes clear from start to finish is that the law, and human obedience to the law, was incapable of doing what we needed: to be justified, to be brought into a right relationship with God. In that sense, Christ ends the law, brings it to a conclusion. It is not that Christ ends our responsibility to God or to our neighbor; it is rather that Christ represents a different way of entering into a right relationship with God. We accept God's gift through faith. For Paul, that is quite different from living under the law, and in that sense the law is over because Christ provides a new and better way. The obedience of faith is not the same as obedience to the law.

Let me try an example. In one family there is an ongoing debate over the meaning of allowance, a weekly payment to the children of the household to be used for purchasing games and books and compact discs. One way to understand allowance is to understand it as payment. If the children perform a set of tasks (clean the room, take out the garbage, mow the lawn) they will be paid. They get what they earn, and if they don't earn it in any given week, they are "punished" by withholding of the allowance. Another way to understand allowance is to understand it as gift and more than gift. In a small way it does what being in the family does in a large way: It comes with the territory, like love and food and shelter. Of course under this system the children are still expected to clean their rooms, take out the garbage, and mow the lawn. But now they do those chores not to receive a reward or to escape the punishment of allowance withheld. They do the chores because those are responsibilities that come with the gifts.

The second way of understanding allowances and chores seems the more mature, the goal toward which the whole family moves as we grow up and grow in responsibility. It is the end toward which the system of rewards and punishments was really moving.

It is also the end, the finish, of that other way of living together. It is therefore a picture of the way responsibility functions for Christians as Paul understands it. We are already gifted with the immeasurable grace of God in Jesus Christ. In him we have food for our souls, shelter against the powers of despair, love that never ends. We do not act responsibly in order to gain those gifts. We act responsibly because we have received those gifts and because responsibility comes with being part of Christ's own family. In such a family, Christ has put an end to the law, an end to achieving or earning our allowance from God—an end to fearing that someday we may be cut off from God's kindness.

Of course, as we have seen from the beginning, this new and better way—the way of faith—is a possibility for Gentiles as well as Jews, and therefore through the gift of faith the one God can offer justification to all of humankind.

With this twofold understanding of the Christ as the end of the law, we can look at the rest of these verses. While elsewhere Paul may argue that sin invariably uses the law for its purposes, or that the law belongs to the old age and Christ to the new age, here he seems rather to make this claim: Everyone has to choose whether to seek God's righteousness through the law or to receive God's righteousness through faith. God has determined to give righteousness as a gift to those who are faithful, so those who seek righteousness some other way have simply taken the wrong path. You cannot have it both ways, and the way of faith is the way in which God has called us to God's own self.

In fact, here Paul argues from the recent history he has observed. Gentiles seem to have taken the right way in greater numbers than Jews have. This isn't an eternal decree; it's the way things have been going recently. Paul will say more about eternal decrees, or divine plans, in the verses that follow.

The quotation that includes the stumbling stone in verse 33 is apparently from Isaiah 28:16. The whole passage in Isaiah is also a passage about righteousness, our righteousness and God's. It may be that Paul heard echoes of the whole passage as he wrote.

> Therefore thus says the Lord GOD,
> See, I am laying in Zion a foundation stone,
> a tested stone,
> a precious cornerstone, a sure foundation:
> "One who trusts will not panic."
> And I will make justice the line,
> and righteousness the plummet.
> (Isa. 28:16–17)

When Paul quotes part of this passage again in Romans 10:11, there is little doubt that the last part of the quotation refers to Jesus: "No one who believes in him will be put to shame." (The NRSV's translation of Isaiah said "One who trusts will not panic.") First Peter 2:6, 8 also understands the stone in which we trust to be Jesus. In the immediate context of Romans 9:33, however, it may be that the rock is the righteousness of faith. Those who trust in it find righteousness; those who trust in the law stumble. (The note in the NRSV margin shows us the alternative.) It may also be that Paul knows the verse can be understood either way, and, as he so often does, he uses the double meaning to his purposes. Those who trust in Christ will not be put to shame. Those who trust in the righteousness of faith will not be put to shame.

In any case, if we are to hear Paul's claim, we need to see that he places before us a choice. Either we continue to seek to enter a right relationship with God by obeying Torah or we receive a right relationship with God through faith. By obeying Torah, Paul means being an observant Jew, keeping kosher, obeying Sabbath laws and purity laws. From the Reformation on, Protestants have often wanted to generalize from Paul's particular claim: Any attempt we make to strive after a right relationship with God, however zealously, is doomed to failure. Every attempt to establish our own relationship to God is idolatrous because we seek to do what only God can do: justify ourselves. A right relationship to God is always a gift, never a wage or an achievement or an accomplishment.

This larger claim about the law has much to commend it. Every Christian testifies that God's goodness to us is an immeasurable gift, far beyond anything we could possibly earn. We do need to remember, though, that for Paul, Christ had not put an end to striving in general but to Torah as the means by which people were to enter into a right relationship to God. Torah was not overcome simply because there is always something wrong with striving. Torah was overcome because God had done something better in Jesus Christ, and we could not have it both ways. (In fact the NRSV translates Rom. 9:31 a bit misleadingly. The Greek does not say that Israel strove for "the righteousness that is based on the law" but that "Israel strove for the law of righteousness." The law in itself is still God's good gift, but in the light of Jesus Christ it has been bested—fulfilled and overcome.)

Furthermore, as we shall see in our discussion of Romans 12—15, the new life under faith by no means meant the end of responsibility toward God or toward the neighbor. But this responsibility grows out of faith; it too is part of God's gift to us.

The familial image again may help. One way of encouraging responsibility in the family is to set up the conditions by which one has to earn approval: If you make your bed and wash the dishes, I will love you. Another way of encouraging responsibility in the family is to begin with love and to say: Because this is a loving family built up in mutual concern and esteem, all of us have responsibilities. Please make your bed and wash the dishes. Either way, one hopes, the chores are done. Either way family members act responsibly.

For Paul, life in faith in some ways looked very much like life under Torah: one did not kill or commit adultery or steal or bear false witness. (We still make the bed and wash the dishes.) But the grounding of that responsibility is different and the purpose of that responsibility is different, too. Acting uprightly is no longer a way of moving into a right relationship with God, but a response to God's right relationship to us.

Righteousness through Faith a Possibility for All
(Romans 10:5–21)

10:5 **Moses writes concerning the righteousness that comes from the law, that "the person who does these things will live by them."** 6 **But the righ-**

teousness that comes from faith says, "Do not say in your heart, 'Who will ascend into heaven?' " (that is, to bring Christ down) [7] "or 'Who will descend into the abyss?' " (that is, to bring Christ up from the dead). [8] But what does it say?

"The word is near you,
on your lips and in your heart"

(that is, the word of faith that we proclaim); [9] because if you confess with your lips that Jesus is Lord and believe in your heart that God raised him from the dead, you will be saved. [10] For one believes with the heart and so is justified, and one confesses with the mouth and so is saved. [11] The scripture says, "No one who believes in him will be put to shame." [12] For there is no distinction between Jew and Greek; the same Lord is Lord of all and is generous to all who call on him. [13] For, "Everyone who calls on the name of the Lord shall be saved."

[14] But how are they to call on one in whom they have not believed? And how are they to believe in one of whom they have never heard? And how are they to hear without someone to proclaim him? [15] And how are they to proclaim him unless they are sent? As it is written, "How beautiful are the feet of those who bring good news!" [16] But not all have obeyed the good news; for Isaiah says, "Lord, who has believed our message?" [17] So faith comes from what is heard, and what is heard comes through the word of Christ.

[18] But I ask, have they not heard? Indeed they have; for
"Their voice has gone out to all the earth,
and their words to the ends of the world."
[19] Again I ask, did Israel not understand? First Moses says,
"I will make you jealous of those who are not a nation;
with a foolish nation I will make you angry."
[20] Then Isaiah is so bold as to say,
"I have been found by those who did not seek me;
I have shown myself to those who did not ask for me."
[21] But of Israel he says: "All day long I have held out my hands to a disobedient and contrary people."

Maybe this passage is the heart of the matter. In verse 12 we read that phrase we remember from the earliest chapters: "there is no distinction." The one God calls all people to God's self through the gift of the one person Jesus Christ. And this gift is received in one way: through faith. "There is no distinction between Jew and Greek; the same Lord is Lord of all and is generous to all who call on him."

Now, however, we see more clearly (we hear more clearly) what faith means. It means speaking, hearing, and believing a word. It means calling on the Lord who has already called us in Jesus Christ. The whole passage stresses the importance of speaking the word of faith and hearing it. Two verses sum up the entire section: "If you confess with your lips that Jesus is Lord and believe in your heart that God raised him from the dead, you will be saved. For one believes with the heart and so is justified, and one confesses with the mouth and so is saved." Notice that the order of events shifts. In the first part of the claim, we speak and then believe. In the second part, we believe and then confess. Faith for Paul is believing in the heart and speaking what we believe. It is hearing the word proclaimed and taking it to heart.

Remember that Paul as apostle is above all preacher. He speaks the word which is in his heart; others take that word to heart. Taking that word to heart *is* faith. It *is* trust in the God who, through Jesus Christ, speaks love and justification to the whole creation.

So often in our time, preaching is simply a long, dull discourse full of truisms and good advice. So often in our time, hearing is halfhearted, or half-eared. We are so used to words as background noise for our thoughts, verbal Muzak. For Paul preaching is announcement, confession, salvation. Hearing is the gift, the opportunity, and the blessing to receive the announcement and rejoice in the salvation. For Paul preaching could never be some dull oral essay simply to be endured. In preaching, life is changed. We are called to faith and through faith to salvation.

Notice, too, that it is not only a matter of hearing good news, it is a matter of obeying good news. In Greek the word for "obey" has as its root the word "hear." But the prefix for "obey" means "under." To obey is literally to "hear under." To obey is to stand under the word you hear; to live out what you receive. To be under the word is to be under orders as well as under grace. From beginning to end, Romans is a letter about the obedience of faith. Paul does not write about faith versus obedience, or faith and then obedience, or obedience that leads to faith. Paul calls the Romans to faith/obedience, obedient faith, faithful obedience.

In order to make his essential claims about faith through hearing, Paul again draws on a considerable amount of Old Testament literature. In verse 8 he quotes the passage from Deuteronomy 30:12–14, about the "word" that is near. If you look up Deuteronomy 30, however, you will notice that it is not the word of faith but the Torah that Moses says is "near." Is Paul taking impossible liberty with the Bible? He is taking considerable liberty, to be sure, but perhaps not impossible liberty. He has just told us that Christ is the end and goal of the law. Torah points us straight to Christ. Therefore, for Paul, the not-very-hidden meaning of scripture is the goal toward which it points: Torah points to Christ. So for a Christian,

Paul apparently thinks, where Moses speaks of the word of the law we can speak of the word that comes in Jesus Christ—the word of faith. It is a bold leap, but a leap of Christian freedom. (The quotation in Rom. 10:8 is actually a combination of Deuteronomy 9 and Deuteronomy 30. In Deuteronomy 9, Moses warns the people not to trust in their own righteousness—in quite a different context than Paul's similar warning. But Paul, who sees the Bible as one great book, not a lot of separate chapters, may well rejoice in combining the warning against one's own righteousness with the assurance that God's righteousness is just as near as the word we hear on Sunday morning or speak to our neighbor on Friday night.)

For us, the claim that the word is near may be a reminder not to try to find God in a dead past or in an impossible future, but to trust that when a faithful word is spoken, God in Christ will be present, near, our refuge and our strength. We are always tempted to center our faith in nostalgia or in longing. Dare we say that we are always tempted to ponder Christ in Galilee or Christ in heaven? The living Christ is the Christ who walked in Galilee and will reign eternally, but is present here, now, among us, for us.

There is one additional way in which this discussion of faith as hearing works. Paul wants to guard against the possibility that the reason Israel has not had faith is that the people have simply never heard the word. (Did you have those discussions in high school or college about whether people in some remote corner of the world who had never heard the gospel were to be condemned for their ignorance? This is an early response to such discussions.) The quotations, especially from Isaiah, but also from the Psalms and Deuteronomy (Rom. 10:18–20), are all used to underline what Paul knows from his own experience. The gospel has indeed been preached to Israel. It is not ignorance that keeps them from faith; it is unfaith, disobedience.

The quotation from Deuteronomy 32 in Romans 10:19 surely reminds us of the quotation from Hosea in Romans 9:25. The "no people" now put to shame the "people." The outsiders shame the insiders. The Gentiles have received what Israel refused. Paul says that surely Israel should be deeply embarrassed. Paul's great hope is just that: Israel will be deeply embarrassed.

THE FINAL HOPE
Romans 11:1–36

The beginning of the discussion of Israel's place in history has foretold the conclusion. For Paul it is inconceivable that God would go back on God's promises. The question has been, How is that promise to be fulfilled? Chapter 11 provides Paul's answer to that question.

God Leaves a Remnant
(Romans 11:1–10)

11:1 I ask, then, has God rejected his people? By no means! I myself am an Israelite, a descendant of Abraham, a member of the tribe of Benjamin. ² God has not rejected his people whom he foreknew. Do you not know what the scripture says of Elijah, how he pleads with God against Israel? ³ "Lord, they have killed your prophets, they have demolished your altars; I alone am left, and they are seeking my life." ⁴ But what is the divine reply to him? "I have kept for myself seven thousand who have not bowed the knee to Baal." ⁵ So too at the present time there is a remnant, chosen by grace. ⁶ But if it is by grace, it is no longer on the basis of works, otherwise grace would no longer be grace.

⁷ What then? Israel failed to obtain what it was seeking. The elect obtained it, but the rest were hardened, ⁸ as it is written,

> "God gave them a sluggish spirit,
>   eyes that would not see
>   and ears that would not hear,
>   down to this very day."

⁹ And David says,

>   "Let their table become a snare and a trap,
>   a stumbling block and a retribution for them;
> ¹⁰ let their eyes be darkened so that they cannot see,
>   and keep their backs forever bent."

In these verses, Paul draws on a rich tradition within Israel's own self-understanding. Time after time in Israel true faith has been kept, not by the majority, but by the minority of Israelites, who have continued to worship and serve the true God.

The quotation in Romans 11:8 seems to combine what Moses says to the Hebrews in the wilderness in Deuteronomy 29:4 and what Isaiah says to Jerusalem in Isaiah 29:10. Remember that Paul has already identified himself with Moses in Romans 9:1–2. Now the words of Moses may seem especially appropriate in their larger context.

> Moses summoned all Israel and said to them: You have seen all that the LORD did before your eyes in the land of Egypt, to Pharaoh and to all his servants and to all his land, the great trials that your eyes saw, the signs, and those great wonders. But to this day the LORD has not given you a mind to understand, or eyes to see, or ears to hear. (Deut. 29:2–4)

Paul believes that God has done great signs and wonders in Jesus Christ and in the church, and yet most of those in Israel do not yet have a mind to understand. Their ears will not hear. Their eyes cannot see. Just like Pharaoh's heart, their hearts are hardened.

In the context of Isaiah 29, Isaiah says that God has provided a vision to Jerusalem but the people treat it like a sealed document. Either they refuse to open the document or they say they are unable to read. If we think of this "sealed document" as a kind of foreshadowing of the gospel with which Paul has been entrusted, we can understand his frustration with Israel and his sense that he stands in the line of the great prophets. Paul has provided the gospel, but most of his fellow Jews treat it like a sealed document. They refuse to open the text. They refuse to open their eyes.

Paul carries this identification with the prophets even further, in two extraordinary ways. First, he himself becomes the primary example of the remnant of Israel, because he, an Israelite, has come to faith through grace. He has accepted what God has done in Jesus Christ. In this Paul identifies himself with Elijah, as at the beginning of chapter 9 he identifies himself with Moses. As Moses and Elijah represented law and prophets for the people of Israel, so Paul—as apostle—represents God's new way for God's new people.

Second, and even more astonishing, Paul identifies Jews who have not accepted Christ with those earlier Israelites who worshiped Baal. Of course, Paul knows that those Jews who have not joined the church continue to worship Yahweh, "the Lord." But, to his way of thinking, their worship of Yahweh is itself idolatrous, because the god they worship is really the god of one nation, a tribal god, just as Baal was the tribal god of Jezebel's people, the Phoenicians. Therefore the new remnant, the people God has set apart for God's own self, are those Jews who know that God is God of all people, and therefore is the God who acts through grace and not as a reward for the works of the law. God is not a god who rewards us for keeping kosher or for having our male babies circumcised. God is not a god for those who by birthright or choice belong to a particular people—the Jews. God is the God of all, without distinction, and the generous way in which God chooses to relate to all is through grace.

It may seem extremely odd that Paul insists that the remnant, the smaller group of Jews who have true faith, is just that group which acknowledges that God is not the God of any remnant or any single community or any nation but the God of all people, and indeed the God of all creation. Those who worship the true God worship the God who cannot possibly be *their* God. My God is not God. Our God is not God. God is God.

As the church, we still have the hardest time distinguishing the claim that we believe faithfully in the one God from the claim that the one God in whom we believe is peculiarly our God—the Christian God, or worse, the Presbyterian God or the Baptist God. The faithful remnant is the community that bears witness to the claim that God is not our God alone but God of all. Even God of those who are not members of the remnant.

We notice, too, that, as always for Paul, the destiny of Israel rests in God's hands. God "foreknew" Israel. The remnant are not just those who have chosen God. They are those whom God has chosen. They are the "elect." This theme of foreknowledge, predestining, and election will be even more important as Paul draws this discussion of Israel's destiny to a close.

Reminder to Gentiles
(Romans 11:11–24)

11:11 So I ask, have they stumbled so as to fall? By no means! But through their stumbling salvation has come to the Gentiles, so as to make Israel jealous. 12 Now if their stumbling means riches for the world, and if their defeat means riches for Gentiles, how much more will their full inclusion mean!

13 Now I am speaking to you Gentiles. Inasmuch then as I am an apostle to the Gentiles, I glorify my ministry 14 in order to make my own people jealous, and thus save some of them. 15 For if their rejection is the reconciliation of the world, what will their acceptance be but life from the dead! 16 If the part of the dough offered as first fruits is holy, then the whole batch is holy; and if the root is holy, then the branches also are holy.

17 But if some of the branches were broken off, and you, a wild olive shoot, were grafted in their place to share the rich root of the olive tree, 18 do not boast over the branches. If you do boast, remember that it is not you that support the root, but the root that supports you. 19 You will say, "Branches were broken off so that I might be grafted in." 20 That is true. They were broken off because of their unbelief, but you stand only through faith. So do not become proud, but stand in awe. 21 For if God did not spare the natural branches, perhaps he will not spare you. 22 Note then the kindness and the severity of God; severity toward those who have fallen, but God's kindness toward you, provided you continue in his kindness; otherwise you also will be cut off. 23 And even those of Israel, if they do not persist in unbelief, will be grafted in, for God has the power to graft them in again. 24 For if you have been cut from what is by nature a wild olive tree and grafted, contrary to nature, into a cultivated olive tree, how much more will these natural branches be grafted back into their own olive tree.

Two themes emerge here. First is the constant reminder that God has not abandoned Israel. The last word is always mercy, and the purpose of hardening is always to lead toward repentance and salvation. The argument begins to point ahead. The mission to the Gentiles is in part undertaken to make the Jews jealous. If, by their refusal to receive Christ through faith, the Jews opened the way to the Gentile mission (in Paul's words, their refusal meant riches for the world, that is, for Gentiles), then, when they do come into the community of faith, how much more that will mean.

Here is our old argument from the lesser to the greater; grace is always greater than judgment, mercy greater than defeat. If in Adam's disobedience all tasted death, how much more will Christ's obedience mean life? If the Jews' rejection of the gospel meant life to the Gentiles, how much more will their acceptance mean? Mercy piled upon mercy.

The second theme is shown in the image or parable of the olive shoot. Interpreters disagree on whether Paul knows very much about how olives actually grow, but the meaning of the picture for the life of the church is clear enough. Those of us who are Gentile Christians were not originally part of the community God called. At the beginning God called Israel. But we have been grafted into that community. (Earlier, remember, Paul tells us that through Jesus Christ we have been adopted as God's own children.) And there is a strong warning to Gentile Christians who may be boasting of their part in God's plan, their acceptance of Jesus Christ. Don't be so sure of yourselves; if Israel fell away, so might you. Don't be too sure about Israel; if God has shown mercy on you Gentiles, how much more may God show mercy on the people of Israel, who are the root, and the natural branches, of God's own olive tree.

Even in our own time, the trouble with certainty about one's own salvation is the tendency to look down on those we are quite sure are not saved. When we do that we boast, not in the Lord, but in ourselves and our own belief, as if *our* belief saved us and not the grace of God. Yet the God who is in Jesus Christ always justifies the ungodly; we are part of God's people not because of our godliness but despite our ungodliness. Further, if God in Jesus Christ has brought *us* into a right relationship with God, there is no limit to what God can do. There is certainly no group of people that we can exclude from God's power and God's mercy. "Do not boast over the branches," says Paul to the Gentile Christians. "Do not boast over Israel."

This is a clear, strong word to all of us Christians who tend to think that we are the ones God has called, leaving the Jews to their own devices. Not at all. God called them first; we are grafted onto them. We can also be sure that the final plan of God's mercy does not forget God's promises to Israel first, and only then to those of us who are Gentile believers.

Restoration
(Romans 11:25–36)

11:25 **So that you may not claim to be wiser than you are, brothers and sisters, I want you to understand this mystery: a hardening has come upon part of Israel, until the full number of the Gentiles has come in.** 26 **And so all Israel will be saved; as it is written,**
> **"Out of Zion will come the Deliverer;**
> **he will banish ungodliness from Jacob."**
> 27 **"And this is my covenant with them,**
> **when I take away their sins."**
28 **As regards the gospel they are enemies of God for your sake; but as regards election they are beloved, for the sake of their ancestors;** 29 **for the gifts and the calling of God are irrevocable.** 30 **Just as you were once disobedient to God but have now received mercy because of their disobedience,** 31 **so they have now been disobedient in order that, by the mercy shown to you, they too may now receive mercy.** 32 **For God has imprisoned all in disobedience so that he may be merciful to all.**
33 **O the depth of the riches and wisdom and knowledge of God! How unsearchable are his judgments and how inscrutable his ways!**
> 34 **"For who has known the mind of the Lord?**
> **Or who has been his counselor?**
> 35 **"Or who has given a gift to him,**
> **to receive a gift in return?"**
36 **For from him and through him and to him are all things. To him be the glory forever. Amen.**

Paul now reinforces the claim of the first three chapters of Romans. There he put it this way: "Since all have sinned and fall short of the glory of God, [all] are now justified by his grace as a gift" (Rom. 3:23–24).

Here he puts it this way: "For God has imprisoned all in disobedience so that he may be merciful to all" (Rom. 11:32).

In chapters 9—11, Paul tells the Romans how it is that God is a God who deals with "all" in wrath and mercy. The question he worries about is this: If God deals in mercy with all, then what has happened to Israel, who first received the promise of that mercy? Does the "all" still include them?

Chapter 11 completes the answer to that question. Of course God's mercy still includes Israel, but God has reversed the order of God's dealing with humankind. Until Jesus Christ, God's mercy was promised first to Israel and only then to the Gentiles. Since Jesus Christ, it is the Gentiles who have come to receive God's mercy through faith, but the promise will now—very soon—be fulfilled to the Jews.

In part, Paul is here speaking out of his own experience. One might not have predicted that Gentiles would enter into this faithful relationship with God before most Jews did, but in fact that is the way it has turned out. In part Paul is speaking theologically: Since God justifies the ungodly, it is only when Israel recognizes its own ungodliness that Israel, too, will be saved. It is only through disobedience that Israel will come to obedience. The gifts and the calling are irrevocable, but what we now know is that they were promised—from the beginning—to the obedience of faith and not to the obedience of the Torah.

Again we see that Paul has made his bold leap as an interpreter. In the great story of Israel's salvation at the exodus it was Pharaoh's heart that was hardened. In the great story of the world's salvation in Jesus Christ it is Israel's heart that has been hardened—but not forever. For now. For a very short now.

We can see here, too, that though Paul is the great apostle to the Gentiles, his larger goal is also to serve God's plan to bring Israel into that right relationship that comes through faith. When the full number of the Gentiles have come in, Israel will be shamed, astonished, enticed to receive the grace of the God who says: "All day long I have held out my hands to you" (Rom. 10:21; Isa. 65:2, paraphrased).

It may even be that one reason Paul is so eager to continue his ministry in Spain is that Spain was the farthest western boundary of the known world. After he has preached the gospel in Spain, Gentiles from the eastern boundary of the Roman Empire to the western will have heard the gospel, and many will have believed. If the Romans can strengthen Paul on his westward trip, they will be hastening the day when the full number of the Gentiles has come in, and Israel will come in, too. (In the portion of Isaiah just before the words Paul quotes about the Redeemer from Zion we read this: "So those in the west shall fear the name of the LORD, and those in the east, his glory." See Isa. 59:19–20 and Rom. 11:26.)

The doxology, the song of praise, which ends this section of Romans (11:36) is not a pious afterthought, a hymn tagged on after the sermon. It sums up everything Paul has claimed from Romans 1:1 through Romans 11:32, and especially Paul's claims in Romans 9—11. God is still God. However unknowable God's plans, they are God's plans and will be fulfilled. Every promise will be accomplished. The final promise is that promise to which the whole epistle points: From God, through God, to God are *all* things. That means all people belong to God, Jews as well as Gentiles; Gentiles as well as Jews. It means that all creation belongs to God as well, and in God's time God will claim God's own.

The structure of Romans 9—11 is remarkable because it begins with an implied curse and ends with a pronounced blessing. Paul begins with his willingness to be cut off for the sake of his Jewish compatriots and ends by praising the God who chooses to cut no one off. Paul is willing to be cut off from Christ for the sake of Israel, but of course God's work in Christ moves to include all creation in God's righteousness. (Compare Rom. 9:1–3 with Rom. 11:33–36.)

Paul's vision was not fulfilled just as he intended. It seems unlikely that he ever got to Spain, and while it is true that great numbers of Gentiles have come to Christian faith from Paul's day till our own, it is not the case that most Jews have been embarrassed into joining the church. Jews and Christians alike claim to be heirs of Abraham, and most Jews do not believe that faith in Christ is the tie that binds people to Abraham and Abraham's God. Moreover a third great faith, Islam, has arisen since Paul's time, also claiming its inheritance from Abraham.

Some Christians still think they can figure out a timetable by which Israel will come overwhelmingly to accept Christ. Other Christians zealously seek to hasten that day by their mission to Jews. Still other Christians are eager to engage in conversation with Jewish neighbors but think that attempts to convert Jews are presumptuous and that both the synagogue and the church, in quite different ways, bear witness to the God of Abraham. Still other Christians are glad to bear witness to their faith but eager to hear the faith of their Jewish neighbors, too. They enter conversation without judging in advance where the conversation will lead, or how opinions and convictions may change.

It is perhaps not surprising that our Jewish neighbors may be more wary of such conversations than we, because many Christians have a commitment to convince and evangelize Jews while very few Jews wish to convert Christians. It is also the case that for us (as for Paul) the existence of the synagogue raises theological questions: Are God's promises to Israel fulfilled in the church or in Judaism, or in both? If Christ is the answer to Israel's ancient hopes, why don't more Jews believe in him as Lord? For most Jews the existence of the churches do not raise theological questions at all. They have always lived as a dispersed minority among Gentiles of various faiths. Furthermore, too often we Christians have not stood strongly against those who treat Judaism with contempt and sometimes treat Jews with unimaginable malice.

It is impossible to guess where Paul would stand in his understanding of twentieth-century Judaism and its relationship to Christian churches. It is clear enough what he understands of God—first century to twenty-first. God is God, whose promises are unfailing. It is God's intent that from God, through God, and to God all things shall find their purpose and their blessing, and all people shall be blessed as well. God will accomplish that, in God's time and in God's way.

That is why Paul can say what we also say and sing and believe: "To God be the glory forever. Amen."

Finally, we can see how the overall structure of Romans includes chapters 9—11. In chapters 1—3, Paul shows how God's judgment falls on all and how God's grace is available to all. He looks first at Gentile sin, and then, just as Jewish people are beginning to boast of their faithfulness to the law, Paul shows that Jews, too, fall short of the glory of God and need God's grace. In chapters 9—11 Paul looks first at Israel's falling away, and then, just as Gentile people are beginning to boast about their place in God's covenant, Paul reminds us that Gentiles, too, are part of God's plan only by mercy—and that that same mercy is extended and will continue to be extended to Israel.

The overall structure of the letter so far can therefore be diagrammed like this:

A.   All have sinned and fall short of the glory of God (not only Gentiles but Jews).
B.   Justification and the gift of the Spirit: for all!
A1. All have sinned and fall short of the glory of God (not only Jews but Gentiles).
B1. Doxology: God is God of all!

We can see how this structure fits our understanding of one reason why Paul writes this letter. Since Jewish Christian communities in Rome need to get along with Gentile Christian communities in Rome, it is essential for Roman Christians to understand that God's plan is to redeem Jews and Gentiles alike. Jews are not to boast because they have been given the law. Gentiles are not to boast because their brothers and sisters and cousins are flocking to the Christian faith in great numbers. All are brought into a right relationship with God who justifies the ungodly. All have sinned; all have been consigned to disobedience. The one God justifies all through the one person Jesus Christ whose mercy is accepted in one way—through the obedience of faith.

With chapter 12, Paul begins to show us how faith lives out its obedience.

5. Faithful Obedience
Romans 12:1–15:13

For Paul, faith and obedience go hand in hand, or more exactly, they are one thing—faithful obedience. Yet, to make his case, he needs to separate them and stress first one aspect of faithful obedience and then the other. For eleven chapters he has stressed *faithful* obedience. Now for the rest of the letter he will stress faithful *obedience*.

TRANSFORMED FOR OBEDIENCE
Romans 12:1–13:14

Being Transformed (Romans 12:1–2)

12:1 **I appeal to you therefore, brothers and sisters, by the mercies of God, to present your bodies as a living sacrifice, holy and acceptable to God, which is your spiritual worship. 2 Do not be conformed to this world, but be transformed by the renewing of your minds, so that you may discern what is the will of God—what is good and acceptable and perfect.**

We do not want to put too much weight on the little word "therefore" in this beginning of Paul's appeal to obedience. Nonetheless, we can see that Paul's concern for the shape of our lives is a great "therefore." We live lives of obedience and love because of the gospel of the God who in Jesus Christ enters into a right relationship with the ungodly and *therefore* calls us into a right relationship with one another.

More directly, the "therefore" follows the great blessing at the end of Romans 11: "From him [God] and through him and to him are all things. To him be the glory forever" (Rom. 11:36). The question Paul addresses in Romans 12:1–2 is, How do we glorify God? That is, How do we worship the one from whom, through whom, and to whom all things are?

The answer is that we worship with our bodies. That is, we worship the God who is all with all that we are. We can see that our distinction between body and spirit is not a distinction Paul would understand: "spiritual worship" or perhaps "logical worship" is what we do with our bodies. Our conduct is our proper sacrifice to God. We are bound to remember Micah 6:6–8.

> "With what shall I come before the LORD,
>   and bow myself before God on high?
> Shall I come before him with burnt offerings,
>   with calves a year old?
> Will the LORD be pleased with thousands of rams,
>   with ten thousands of rivers of oil?
> Shall I give my firstborn for my transgression,
>   the fruit of my body for the sin of my soul?"
> He has told you, O mortal, what is good;
>   and what does the LORD require of you
> but to do justice, and to love kindness,
>   and to walk humbly with your God?

Remember that Paul believes that, in Jesus Christ, history shifted forever. The old age of sin and death, where we tried but failed to obey the law, has passed away. A new age based on God's gifts and our faith has begun. The verse "Do not be conformed to this world" could just as well be translated "Do not be conformed to this age." That is, "Live as citizens of the new age of faithful obedience. Be who you really are."

The command to "be transformed" uses the Greek word that has come into English as "metamorphosis." Butterflies may be overused as symbols of the Christian life, but the metamorphosis from caterpillar to butterfly is not a bad symbol of what Paul hopes for Christians. In baptism we are moved from our old citizenship and our old shape to the new shape of faithfulness. We move from the old age of sin and the law to the new age of grace and faith and faithful obedience.

One way to understand Paul's own life is as a story of metamorphosis. He was a persecutor of Christians. Now he is a Christian. He was an enemy of Christ. Now he is Christ's apostle. He has been transformed. The Roman Christians have also been transformed. Paul calls the Romans to acknowledge their transformation. His letter calls us to think about our own loyalties, the changes we undergo when we pledge our allegiance to Christ alone, the Lord of God's new age.

The metamorphosis we undergo as Christians is this: Our minds are made new. That of course doesn't just mean that we have a lot of new information, as our minds might be renewed by learning geography or biology. It means that what we want and intend and hope for and trust in is all made new. Transformed.

As transformed people, the Roman Christians are asked to "discern what is the will of God . . ." The RSV translation seems stronger here: "to prove what is the will of God." That means both to discern God's will, or to discover it, and to prove what is God's will in our own experience. To put it to the test. The proof of the pudding is in the eating. The proof of God's will is in the living. What God's will turns out to be is what is "good and acceptable and perfect." If we obediently live lives that are good, acceptable, and (moving toward) the perfect, we will discover that those are the lives that serve God's kingdom, that worship and glorify God.

In the next chapters Paul shows in some detail what such faithfully obedient lives look like.

The verb with which Paul begins this section of his letter is translated "I appeal." It also means "I beg" or "I beseech" (and sometimes even "I comfort"). One might think that as an apostle Paul could say "I order" or "I command," but even in churches he knows well, churches he founded, Paul beseeches rather than gives orders. The term suggests Paul's close involvement in the lives of his fellow Christians. He cares deeply about them and shares profoundly in their faith, as they share in his. Using the term is a way of living out Paul's wish at the very beginning of the letter: "For I am longing to see you so that I may share with you some spiritual gift to strengthen you—or rather so that we may be mutually encouraged by each other's faith, both yours and mine" (Rom. 1:11–12).

The apostle doesn't give the Roman Christians orders. He begs them lovingly to live out lives of loving obedience. He trusts the faithfulness of Christians enough to spell out for them a life that is their obligation—and their gift—as those who follow Christ as Lord.

Romans 12:1–2 is a word of encouragement and direction for all of us, not just for first-century Roman Christians. All of us are always in danger of pretending to live in the "old age," where we loved sin and set up rules to overcome our sin and then broke the rules and sinned again. All of us are in danger of worshiping with our piety and not with our bodies, of bringing Christ our prayers but not our obedience.

The Transformed Life in the Church
(Romans 12:3–13)

12:3 **For by the grace given to me I say to everyone among you not to think of yourself more highly than you ought to think, but to think with sober judg-**

ment, each according to the measure of faith that God has assigned. [4] For as in one body we have many members, and not all the members have the same function, [5] so we, who are many, are one body in Christ, and individually we are members one of another. [6] We have gifts that differ according to the grace given to us: prophecy, in proportion to faith; [7] ministry, in ministering; the teacher, in teaching; [8] the exhorter, in exhortation; the giver, in generosity; the leader, in diligence; the compassionate, in cheerfulness.

[9] Let love be genuine; hate what is evil, hold fast to what is good; [10] love one another with mutual affection; outdo one another in showing honor. [11] Do not lag in zeal, be ardent in spirit, serve the Lord. [12] Rejoice in hope, be patient in suffering, persevere in prayer. [13] Contribute to the needs of the saints; extend hospitality to strangers.

We can oversimplify and say that in this first set of pleas Paul makes to the Romans in these chapters he is speaking of life within the church (Rom. 12:3–13) and that the second set of pleas deals with the relationship between church members and outsiders (Rom. 12:14–13:7). There is some overlapping; the lines are a little fuzzy, but in the main we can see Paul moving from one set of issues to the other.

"Love" is the major gift by which all Christians live—with one another first, but also in the world. Love, as we shall see, does not mean romantic love or even always deep affectionate feeling for the other. It does mean treating the other with fairness, compassion, and fellow feeling.

What Paul says about love in 1 Corinthians 13 is helpful for understanding his discussion of love in other letters like this one. In fact, the NRSV translation of Romans 12:9 may mislead us a bit here. Paul does not include any verb in this sentence; "Let love be genuine" might better be translated "Love is genuine" or "Love shows no hypocrisy." Then the rest of the paragraph describes what genuine love looks like, just as 1 Corinthians 13 shows what love looks like. In Romans, love looks like the opposite of hypocrisy. It does what it says and acts out what it believes. It is faith lived out in obedience.

One thing that genuine love means is mutual respect among Christians. Paul talks about such love, both here and in 1 Corinthians, by talking about the church as the body of Christ. When Paul writes in this way he does not mean that the church is *like* Christ's body. He means the church *is* Christ's body. For Paul, Christ's glorified body is with God, but Christ's body is also the church. Christ is Lord of the church. Christ's Spirit animates the church. The church lives out Christ in the world.

That is very hard for us to grasp and harder for us to evade. If we are to understand ourselves as Paul would understand us, we are not only

Christ's servants or Christ's followers: we *are* Christ's members, to one another and to the world outside as well.

Of course, we are not the whole of Christ's body, not one of us: not the deacon nor the minister nor the priest nor the church school teacher nor the church treasurer. Together we are Christ's body, but one by one we are only members of the body, and therefore we need one another in order to be who we are, in order to be Christ.

Paul writes about the different kinds of people who are apparently some of the folk in the churches in Rome; surely not every kind of Christian but some kinds of Christians—prophets, ministers (the Greek is "deacons," and we're not sure exactly what such deacons did), teachers, exhorters, leaders or administrators, and those who engage in acts of compassion. There is no evidence that any of these are ordained or "set apart." Every Christian has his or her gifts and responsibilities, and each is to exercise those responsibilities for the sake of Christ's whole body.

It is not clear how our versions of ordination would fit with Paul's vision of the church. Because we live in the midst of a long history he had not expected, and the church is an institution among institutions, there may be no escaping the value of ordination and office in the churches. What Paul clearly would not have imagined was that somehow an ordained person would be expected to exhibit all the gifts of ministry. Paul would not have expected other Christians to demand so much of any one Christian or to hand to one person responsibilities that could be shared mutually. Paul would not have expected any one Christian to take on as much power as some clergypeople possess. Paul's own authority was always held in mutuality, and the church was an extension of Christ's will, not an extension of the pastor's.

Moreover, Paul reminds the Roman Christians that because all of them need one another and because all of them find their meaning and purpose in Christ, there is to be no boasting of one Christian over another. Faithful worship of the living God means loving our fellow Christians, and that means no bragging, no pushing about, no lording it over one another. How can we lord it over one another when we have one Lord?

Paul's words remind us of what Jesus tells his disciples (and future church leaders) in Matthew 23:8–10:

> But you are not to be called rabbi, for you have one teacher, and you are all students [literally, brothers]. And call no one your father on earth, for you have one Father—the one in heaven. Nor are you to be called instructors, for you have one instructor, the Messiah.

It is not quite clear what Paul means when he says the Romans should think of themselves with "sober judgment, each according to the measure of faith that God has assigned" (12:3), because usually Paul doesn't think of faith as being a matter of degree: You have it or you don't. Maybe he means "according to the diverse gifts by which you act faithfully." There is one faith, but there are different kinds of obedience according to your own calling and responsibility.

The significance of this claim that we are Christ's body for today's church can hardly be overstated. We still live with distinctions and pretensions: We pretend that there are super Christians (often called clergy) and regular Christians. We pretend that those who have one church office are more important than those who have another and that officeholders are obviously more valuable than those who have no office. We take on titles and uniforms and honorary degrees and look just like the outside world with our pomp and our prestige. Shame on us. We are called to be transformed by the making new of our whole minds; when we are made new, we shall see how much we need one another, how much we belong to one another, how little ground we have for boasting.

Now with a series of imperatives, commands, Paul spells out what genuine love looks like. He spells out what it means for members of the body of Christ to be members one of another. Christians serve the Lord and honor each other. The two responsibilities go together: faithful obedience. Verse 12 sums up briefly the implications of the whole great mediation on hope found in Romans 8: "Rejoice in hope, be patient in suffering, persevere in prayer."

Being the body of Christ also means direct, practical care for one another. "The saints" are fellow Christians, and Paul enjoins the church to provide practical help for Christians in need. (He may also be thinking of the needs of the saints in Jerusalem for whom he is collecting an offering.) The command to hospitality reminds us that people often traveled about the Roman Empire. The long list of Christians living in Rome whom Paul knew from other places in the Roman Empire in Romans 16 further confirms how much Christians were apt to move about in those days. Therefore one job of Christians was to welcome other Christians. Paul, of course, hopes that soon the Roman Christians will also welcome him.

Sometimes in our honorable zeal for right theology and great causes we can forget that faithful obedience also involves daily kindnesses. We do not have to choose between the great political concerns of our time and the immediate needs of our own church people. Every Christian congregation will want to provide resources for the needy in their midst. And even in a time when we are afraid of strangers, we will want to discover forms of hospitality that help people feel welcome in places far from home.

One college, for example, sends to its graduates lists of fellow graduates who are glad to provide hospitality to wandering alums and their families. Our churches might learn from this show of fellow feeling and provide networks of support and kindness.

In a time when so many people are homeless, Christian hospitality may take on an even broader meaning. Through a coalition, churches in one community, for instance, take turns providing shelter and food to homeless people, and church members share the responsibility for feeding and visiting, for hospitality. In that shared ministry Christ's body has many members: the Episcopal congregations are members, as are the Presbyterian and the Baptist.

The Transformed Life in the World
(Romans 12:14–13:7)

12:14 **Bless those who persecute you; bless and do not curse them. [15] Rejoice with those who rejoice, weep with those who weep. [16] Live in harmony with one another; do not be haughty, but associate with the lowly; do not claim to be wiser than you are. [17] Do not repay anyone evil for evil, but take thought for what is noble in the sight of all. [18] If it is possible, so far as it depends on you, live peaceably with all. [19] Beloved, never avenge yourselves, but leave room for the wrath of God; for it is written, "Vengeance is mine, I will repay, says the Lord." [20] No, "if your enemies are hungry, feed them; if they are thirsty, give them something to drink; for by doing this you will heap burning coals on their heads." [21] Do not be overcome by evil, but overcome evil with good.**

13:1 Let every person be subject to the governing authorities; for there is no authority except from God, and those authorities that exist have been instituted by God. [2] Therefore whoever resists authority resists what God has appointed, and those who resist will incur judgment. [3] For rulers are not a terror to good conduct, but to bad. Do you wish to have no fear of the authority? Then do what is good, and you will receive its approval; [4] for it is God's servant for your good. But if you do what is wrong, you should be afraid, for the authority does not bear the sword in vain! It is the servant of God to execute wrath on the wrongdoer. [5] Therefore one must be subject, not only because of wrath but also because of conscience. [6] For the same reason you also pay taxes, for the authorities are God's servants, busy with this very thing. [7] Pay to all what is due them—taxes to whom taxes are due, revenue to whom revenue is due, respect to whom respect is due, honor to whom honor is due.

The first paragraph of this section (Rom. 12:14–21) clearly includes rules for relationships both with fellow Christians and with "outsiders." Paul's major concern here, however, is how to get along with those who are not Christians. The passage is both realistic and faithful to Paul's gospel. It is realistic because it recognizes that sometimes it is not up to us whether our neighbors will be our friends or not. We are responsible for our own behavior, but we cannot guarantee that others will treat us as we treat them. It is realistic because it acknowledges that how we behave will affect our reputation, and while reputation is a minor concern for Christians, it is a concern. It is realistic because it acknowledges that faithful obedience will often meet with opposition and perhaps even persecution.

Romans 12:14–21 is also theologically faithful because it calls Christians to go beyond the "natural" desire to get back at those who do us harm. As in Jesus' teaching in the Sermon on the Mount, Paul tells the Roman Christians not to retaliate when evil is done them. They are not to retaliate for two reasons. First, judgment, or justice, is God's business and not ours. Paul never doubts for a minute that God *will* work justice, but because of that, we can faithfully and patiently refuse to be our own avengers. The verse Paul quotes in Romans 12:20 is from Deuteronomy 32:35, part of a passage in which God promises to deliver God's people from enemies. Second, by doing good we may in fact overcome evil, turn evil to the good. The passage Paul quotes about "coals of fire" is from Proverbs 25:21–22. In its context the passage seems to mean that by doing good, faithful people bring their enemies to repentance and purified lives. Paul says that by doing good to others, Christians work good, increase good in the lives of others. Sometimes, at least, if we do unto others as we would have them do to us, they *will* treat us more kindly and generously.

The Society of Friends, the Quakers, have a reminder that we should look for what is of God in every person. Paul would suggest that we serve what is of God in every person. Sometimes that other person's godliness will respond to our kindness, but even when it does not, judgment is God's business and not ours. (Remember that this is the God who moves through judgment and mercy to bring the whole creation to God's self. God will be God and no persecution or persecutors will stop that.)

The second major discussion in Paul's portrayal of the obedient life in the world is the discussion of the relationship to rulers in 13:1–7. The heart of the argument is clear enough. God who created the world also orders the world. Part of that order is government, and government exists to keep us from hurting one another. Therefore the obligation of the Christian is to be a good citizen, paying taxes and obeying the laws.

We need to remember that Paul writes this letter as the citizen of a great empire but also as a member of a very small, minority community— the Christian church. He had seen fellow believers persecuted, and would himself before long be martyred. For the most part, Christians were not powerful people in the empire. They did not vote or influence policy; rules were made far away and passed down.

Furthermore, Paul has every expectation that Christ will return soon. The idea of ongoing opposition to government makes little sense if government itself is about to end.

Therefore Romans 13 is generally helpful but not always specifically helpful. It does not tell us what to do when we as citizens of a democracy can help make the laws, not simply choose whether to obey them. It does not really raise the question of the proper response to tyranny. It does not tell us what Christians should do in the face of Nazi power, or in the face of legal segregation.

In the New Testament itself there is a striking contrast between the understanding of government power as found in Romans and in the book of Revelation, where John of Patmos claims that imperial power comes from Satan, not from God. In the Bible as a whole, we have Paul urging that we respect authority; we also have Elijah and Jeremiah condemning authorities. Christians looking for an easy answer to the question of how to be good citizens will not find such answers in the Bible. Different biblical writers bring different insights to different situations.

What the Bible does protest, from cover to cover, is idolatry. Paul has made clear from the start that one cannot confuse anything less than god with God. Paul may encourage obedience to rulers, but he would never encourage total allegiance to an emperor. Emperors were servants of God but not gods. Other Christian writers like John of Patmos think that even that gives the emperor more than his due.

For Christians of our time seeking to understand the responsibilities of citizenship, Romans 13 is one resource, but not the only one. Furthermore, Paul's last word still leaves us to make important decisions about their implications: "Pay to all what is due them . . . respect to whom respect is due, honor to whom honor is due."

In the twentieth century, one of the striking instances of the struggle with faithfulness in the light of political tyranny is the story of Dietrich Bonhoeffer, a German pastor and theologian during the Third Reich.

Bonhoeffer decided he had to choose between a kind of Christian purity that refused to fight authority, even tyrannical authority, and his responsibility to history and to history's God. He had to face that question in ways that would not have occurred to Paul, who thought history was about to end. Bonhoeffer wrote these words, which pose a problem to any simple affirmation of Romans 13 as a guide for our own citizenship:

> The ultimate question for a responsible man to ask is not how he is to extricate himself heroically from the affair, but how the coming generation is to live. It is only from this question, with its responsibility toward history, that fruitful solutions can come, even if for the time being they are very humiliating. (See Eberhard Bethge, *Dietrich Bonhoeffer*, 702.)

After much wrestling with his own Christian convictions, Bonhoeffer became part of a conspiracy to overthrow Hitler. Just before World War II ended, Bonhoeffer was executed.

Law and Faithful Obedience
(Romans 13:8–10)

13:8 Owe no one anything, except to love one another; for the one who loves another has fulfilled the law. ⁹ The commandments, "You shall not commit adultery; You shall not murder; You shall not steal; You shall not covet"; and any other commandment, are summed up in this word, "Love your neighbor as yourself." ¹⁰ Love does no wrong to a neighbor; therefore, love is the fulfilling of the law.

In Romans 12:9–13, Paul has shown us what love looks like positively: honoring others, showing hospitality. Here he shows us what love looks like negatively: Love is *not* doing wrong to the other. He catches the exact function of the commandments he quotes: They are "shall nots." They set the limits of faithful behavior. So, too, in this letter, the law, for all its greatness and graciousness, is primarily the way God sets limits on our behavior, summed up in "You shall not covet," the commandment Adam violated when he coveted the fruit of the tree.

In the light of the commandments, love is not so much what we do positively (as it is in 1 Corinthians 13); it is what we refuse, for the neighbor's sake, to do. We refuse to commit adultery; we refuse to murder; we refuse to steal; we refuse to covet. Because love also sets all these limits for faithful people, love is the fullness of the law. Love sums up the law.

One way of understanding some Jewish leaders of the first century was that they saw their job as beginning with the Ten Commandments, and then elaborating those commandments so that no one would slip. In order to help the faithful, they added examples and exceptions and applications, so that no one would have doubts, for example, about what he or she could do on the Sabbath. Paul works in just the opposite way. Instead of elaborating the Ten Commandments into hundreds, he condenses them to one. Neither the rabbis nor Paul would say that anything goes or that it is up to each of us to figure out our own morality. Both are trying to uphold responsible obedience to the will of God for the sake of the neighbor.

It is also striking that when Paul comes to sum up "the law," what he sums up is not the series of commandments about our relationship to God (the so-called first table of the law) but the series of commandments about our relationship to our neighbors (the second table of the law). Perhaps that is because Romans 1—8 as a whole is really Paul's elaboration of the first table of the law, the claim that God is one and that there is no other. As we have continually seen, for Paul this one God revealed in the First Commandment is the God revealed in Jesus Christ for the redemption of the whole world.

For Paul, therefore, love is the fulfillment of the law, when the law is understood as the list of commandments that regulate our relationships with other people. However, for Paul, love is also more than the fullness of the law. As 1 Corinthians shows, love is the highest gift and the more excellent way. It does what the law does—and how much more!

For Christians today, however, Paul's reminder that love fulfills the law and does not annul the law is a healthy reminder. Future historians, watching our television programs in their archives, especially the commercials, will be convinced that we are above all a "feel good" society. What pleases me, I will do. What I want, I will get. Acquire and exploit seem to be the bywords.

Faithful obedience reminds us that love does not mean doing whatever feels good to me. It means—at the very least—living up to the law, which will not do the neighbor harm. Love may be more than that, but it is never less than that. "If it feels good, do it," needs to be corrected: "If it does harm, don't."

What Time Is It?
(Romans 13:11–14)

13:11 **Besides this, you know what time it is, how it is now the moment for you to wake from sleep. For salvation is nearer to us now than when we became believers;** [12] **the night is far gone, the day is near. Let us then lay aside the works of darkness and put on the armor of light;** [13] **let us live honorably**

as in the day, not in reveling and drunkenness, not in debauchery and licentiousness, not in quarreling and jealousy. [14] Instead, put on the Lord Jesus Christ, and make no provision for the flesh, to gratify its desires.

The claim Paul makes here about God's future for us is a claim every Christian can affirm. Salvation is nearer now than when we first believed. Not only does time move on, but God's strong, sovereign power moves toward its concluding act. Salvation is nearer now because the time grows shorter. Salvation is nearer now because it presses closer upon us. We feel its presence and its power. We do not know either how God's timetable works or how God's strength makes itself known. We do know that salvation draws ever more close.

These verses bring us back to the beginning of Paul's exhortation in Romans 12:1–2. "Do not be conformed to this world." Remember of which age you are a citizen. Paul's image for the time in which we live is the image of the dawn. Night still lurks at the corner of the universe, but, in fact, through Jesus Christ, day is triumphant. Because we live in faithful obedience to Jesus Christ, we will put off the clothes that belong to night and put on daytime armor.

Partly, Paul is recalling the Romans to their baptism, where they put off their clothes before they were lowered into the baptismal water and afterward put on white robes as a sign of their incorporation in the body of Christ. It is the great reminder to which Paul so often returns. "Who are you? You are first of all that person who has put on Jesus Christ. You wear your identity when you wear his name."

There is a kind of small parable enclosed in these verses. Daytime is the time of sober and courageous behavior, the time of faithful obedience. Nighttime is when we're apt to fall into our worst habits, bickering and carousing, and having feuds in the church or with our neighbors. Put on your daytime behavior! Put on Jesus Christ, who is light. Be who you are. We remember Paul's words about baptism: "How can we who died to sin go on living in it?" (Rom. 6:2).

We remember that for Paul the "flesh" is not our selves as sexual but our selves as selfish. Living in the flesh includes not only licentiousness but quarreling and jealousy. Living in the flesh includes both selfish sexuality and selfish willfulness. Living in the "flesh" is living in the old age, the age of night. Living in Christ is living in the new age, the age of the Spirit, the age of light. Dawn is breaking! Put on your morning clothes.

In his *Confessions*, Augustine tells us that he had long been pondering whether he should become a Christian and had asked God to bring him into faithful obedience, only "not yet." One day he happened to overhear a child in the house next to his garden playing a game and crying: "Take, read. Take, read." Augustine picked up the New Testament that was lying on the garden table and found it open to these very words from Paul: "Not in reveling and drunkenness, not in debauchery and licentiousness, not in quarreling and jealousy. Instead, put on the Lord Jesus Christ, and make no provision for the flesh, to gratify its desires" (Rom. 13:13–14; *Confessions* VIII, 8).

From that time on, Augustine determined to be faithful and obedient, to live as a citizen of the light. His story reminds us that the salvation that dawned in Jesus Christ can dawn for each person at that moment God provides. We remember our baptism and hold fast the light. Or we learn of Christ and receive the light in faith. All around us the forces of darkness make their last stand against God and God's Christ, but the light shines in the darkness, and the darkness will not overcome it. We are called to serve the light—we are allowed to serve the light, in the obedience of faith.

OBEDIENT WELCOME
Romans 14:1–15:13

Now Paul moves to a particular example of what it means to live in the light and not to serve the flesh. Some interpreters think Paul is simply drawing on his long experience as an apostle to warn the Romans against behavior he has seen elsewhere. Others think that Paul knows enough about the Roman churches to know that his warnings apply quite directly to them. I think these verses are so specific and direct that Paul has some information about what is happening in Rome. We have seen, and will see again when we look at chapter 16, that Paul knows a number of Christians in Rome, and we can guess that they have given him some idea of what is happening here. My guess is that part of what is going on there is that predominantly Gentile house churches are having to learn to get along with predominantly Jewish house churches, and vice versa.

The Weak and the Strong and Judgment
(Romans 14:1–12)

14:1 **Welcome those who are weak in faith, but not for the purpose of quarreling over opinions. 2 Some believe in eating anything, while the weak eat only vegetables. 3 Those who eat must not despise those who abstain, and** those who abstain must not pass judgment on those who eat; for God has welcomed them. [4] Who are you to pass judgment on servants of another? It is before their own lord that they stand or fall. And they will be upheld, for the Lord is able to make them stand.

[5] Some judge one day to be better than another, while others judge all days to be alike. Let all be fully convinced in their own minds. [6] Those who observe the day, observe it in honor of the Lord. Also those who eat, eat in honor of the Lord, since they give thanks to God; while those who abstain, abstain in honor of the Lord and give thanks to God.

[7] We do not live to ourselves, and we do not die to ourselves. [8] If we live, we live to the Lord, and if we die, we die to the Lord; so then, whether we live or whether we die, we are the Lord's. [9] For to this end Christ died and lived again, so that he might be Lord of both the dead and the living.

[10] Why do you pass judgment on your brother or sister? Or you, why do you despise your brother or sister? For we will all stand before the judgment seat of God. [11] For it is written,

"As I live, says the Lord, every knee shall bow to me,
    and every tongue shall give praise to God."
[12] So then, each of us will be accountable to God.

The theme of welcome runs throughout Romans 14. "Welcome those who are weak in faith," our passage begins (14:1). God has welcomed both the meat eaters and the vegetarians, it continues (14:3). In Romans 15:7 Paul will bring the theme to its conclusion: "Welcome one another, therefore, just as Christ has welcomed you, for the glory of God."

If I am right in thinking that Paul writes in response to what he knows about the Romans, one thing he knows is this: they need to be more welcoming of one another.

We cannot be quite sure who the strong-in-faith Christians and the weak-in-faith Christians are. Paul seems to use the words in almost the opposite way of our usual understanding. Usually we think of strong Christians as those who have very clear rules that they loyally obey and weak Christians as those who seem less concerned with having regulations for every aspect of behavior. But Paul suggests that those who are strong in faith find both freedom and obedience in that faith and do not need so long a set of rules to strengthen their Christianity. Those who are weak in faith may not think faith in itself quite sufficient to give them guidelines to obedience. They are helped by a set of particular rules.

It seems that, in this case, the particular rules include not eating any meat and observing particular holy days, perhaps for fasting and prayer. If the "weak in faith" ate only kosher food and observed the Sabbath, we could be quite sure that they were the Jewish Christians and that the strong in faith were the Gentile Christians who were not worried about traditions brought from their past.

However, it is not entirely clear that the distinction Paul draws is primarily a distinction between Jewish and Gentile Christians. There is no clear evidence of Jewish vegetarianism in Rome of the first century. It may also be that some Christians refused to eat meat because most meat sold in those days was sold at the temple, where the animals that provided the meat had first been used in sacrifices to pagan gods. (First Corinthians, in chapters 8 and 10, has a long discussion of whether Christians can eat meat sacrificed to idols.) Of course, both Gentile and Jewish Christians could have such scruples, and both could strictly observe certain holy days.

A contemporary rabbi made another suggestion. This rabbi maintains the rules for kosher food. When he is invited to join Gentiles at a restaurant, he always orders from the vegetarian menu, because vegetarian meals run little danger of violating kosher rules. Perhaps, he suggests, when Jewish Christians and Gentile Christians came together in Rome for communal suppers, the Jewish Christians insisted on eating vegetarian because there was little danger that any kosher rules had been violated in the cooking of vegetables.

My own guess is based on my reading of the whole book of Romans and on the description of a Christianity influenced by Judaism in Galatians 4:9–10 and Colossians 2:16. My guess is that some of the Jewish Christians who have returned to Rome bring with them strict vegetarian menus and the strict observance of certain days.

Either for this reason, or because of differences over kosher dietary rules, or for reasons we cannot discover, there is some tension within the Christian community when people from different house churches come together to eat. What kind of meals can they have? Do they have to have a vegetarian menu? Do they have to avoid this day or that day because the Jewish Christians fast on that day?

Paul's first word is that all the Roman Christians are to welcome one another (but not just so that they can have a family feud). They are to welcome one another because God is the great welcomer, the one whose arms are always open. (The father's arms are open to the prodigal coming in from the far country and to the older brother standing out there in the fields.) In Romans, when Paul talks about what God has done for people in Jesus Christ, he mainly says that God has justified, made righteous, rightwised those who have faith. Here is another way of talking about what God has done: God has welcomed Gentile and Jew into God's family, God's household.

Paul puts it another way: all are servants of the Lord, and to despise the servant is to despise the Lord. To despise the Lord is simply impossible for Christians. Notice how seldom Paul talks about wrong behavior. He talks about impossible behavior, what Christians cannot possibly do.

Paul has two requirements for the way in which "stronger" and "weaker" Christians should get along with each other. First, they are not to judge each other. Second, the strong are not to cause the weak to stumble.

The verses before us, Romans 14:1–12, deal with the issue of judging. The overall claim is clear enough: no Christian has the right to condemn another Christian for practicing Christianity in ways that are different from one's own. Paul makes his case for mutual acceptance (welcoming) in three ways.

He makes his case, in part, by telling the Roman Christians to think about their own practice. (He did this earlier in the letter when he told them to think about the way they pray "Abba . . . Father" in worship. Their practice is a sign that they are indeed God's children.) Here Paul reminds them again of the way they pray. Those who are willing to eat meat nonetheless say grace before they eat a meal. Those who abstain from meat say grace over their rice and beans. What counts is the fact that vegetarians and meat eaters alike thank the same God, not that different casseroles sit on different plates.

Paul makes his case by the reminder that our lives are not our own. They come from God, and they return to God. In his death and resurrection, Jesus Christ claimed lordship over all creation and over all people: those who eat meat and those who don't; those who keep fast days and those who keep right on eating. If Christ is Lord of all these people, what right have some to look down their noses at others? So often Paul's greatest theological affirmations pop up right in the middle of the most everyday discussions. Here he is worrying about the menu at church suppers and how Christians can stop feuding over cuisine, and he gives the Romans a word that has sustained faithful people from that day until this, and will do so until kingdom come: "We do not live to ourselves, and we do not die to ourselves. If we live, we live to the Lord, and if we die, we die to the Lord; so then, whether we live or whether we die, we are the Lord's" (14:7–8).

In my years as pastor, I have returned time after time to two affirmations from Paul's letter to the Romans. The first is the great passage written to encourage Christians in the time of persecution, Romans 8:31–39, with the reminder that nothing will be able to separate us from the love of God in Christ Jesus our Lord. The second is this passage, written to settle a little family feud about the menu at church suppers. The context seems so ordinary and the text so extraordinary. Yet what the text insists is that all our living and our dying, from the most everyday to the most astonishing, are in God's care and mercy—the care and mercy we see in Jesus Christ.

In some ways the text is reticent. There is no discussion here of the nature of our lives beyond death, no description of the kingdom to come. There is the assurance that we belong to God—in life and in death—and that therefore we belong to one another: in life and in death. We believe in the communion of saints because we believe in the God who brings us into community with God and with one another. The text is so reticent, yet so bold in hope.

Finally, Paul makes his case against Christians judging other Christians by the reminder that God is judge of all, and that judgment belongs to God alone. We are reminded of Jesus' word in the Sermon on the Mount: "Do not judge, so that you may not be judged" (Matt. 7:1). The judge we need to fear and honor is God. We can also be sure that God's judgment does not include eternal concern over what we eat or what days we refrain from eating. By contrasting our judgment to God's, Paul makes clear that God's ways are not our ways and that what we argue about, split churches over, and fire ministers for, may be of no account in the light of God's astonishing judgment and more astonishing grace.

Not surprisingly, the context of the passage that Paul quotes from Isaiah also confirms this stress on God's unique ability to judge and redeem:

> By myself I have sworn,
>   from my mouth has gone forth in righteousness
>   a word that shall not return:
> "To me every knee shall bow,
>   every tongue shall swear."
>
> Only in the LORD, it shall be said of me,
>   are righteousness and strength.
>   (Isa. 45:23–24)

When Christians judge one another, we pretend that righteousness and strength are *ours*. We commit the worst idolatry of all: we take over God's job. We make ourselves into gods.

Stumbling
(Romans 14:13–23)

14:13 **Let us therefore no longer pass judgment on one another, but resolve instead never to put a stumbling block or hindrance in the way of another.** [14] **I know and am persuaded in the Lord Jesus that nothing is unclean in it-**

self; but it is unclean for anyone who thinks it unclean. [15] If your brother or sister is being injured by what you eat, you are no longer walking in love. Do not let what you eat cause the ruin of one for whom Christ died. [16] So do not let your good be spoken of as evil. [17] For the kingdom of God is not food and drink but righteousness and peace and joy in the Holy Spirit. [18] The one who thus serves Christ is acceptable to God and has human approval. [19] Let us then pursue what makes for peace and for mutual upbuilding. [20] Do not, for the sake of food, destroy the work of God. Everything is indeed clean, but it is wrong for you to make others fall by what you eat; [21] it is good not to eat meat or drink wine or do anything that makes your brother or sister stumble. [22] The faith that you have, have as your own conviction before God. Blessed are those who have no reason to condemn themselves because of what they approve. [23] But those who have doubts are condemned if they eat, because they do not act from faith; for whatever does not proceed from faith is sin.

What Paul recommends here is fairly clear. It is one thing for those who are "strong in faith" to eat meat and skip fast days. It is quite another for them to entice the "weak in faith" to do the same.

The strong in faith are quite right, says Paul, in thinking that neither diet nor fasting commend us to God. What we eat and what we drink make no difference as far as God's welcome is concerned. God welcomes those who are kosher and those who are not, vegetarians and meat eaters, Sabbath keepers and Sabbath breakers, those who observe holy days and those who go to work as usual. However, the strong in faith are obliged not to cause the weak in faith to do what is against their own conscience. The weak do violate their understanding of faith when they break dietary rules or fail to observe their religious calendars. They are not acting out of faith, but giving in to temptation, or going along with the crowd. Notice that exactly the same act can be sin or not sin. Eating meat is not sin for those whose faith does not require a vegetarian diet. Eating meat is sin for those whose faith is that God requires abstaining from meat.

The clearest sin is when meat eaters serve up roast lamb to the vegetarians they have invited for dinner. The clearest sin is when the strong in faith invite the weak in faith to come to a picnic on a day that the "weak" think should be a day of fasting. Then some Christians are causing other Christians to stumble, to violate their own consciences.

We can see what Paul's advice would probably mean in practice for the Roman Christians. If a house church consisting entirely of meat eaters got together for supper, there was no sin in serving meat. But if two house churches shared a common meal, let it be a vegetarian meal, lest the vegetarians be tempted to violate their own understanding of faith. Likewise there should be no citywide Christian supper on one of those days that some Christians observed as a fast day. Hold the meal on the next night or the next week.

Beyond the immediate application, Paul's final word on this subject strikes us as immeasurably thought provoking: "Whatever does not proceed from faith is sin."

Though this is not presented strictly as a definition of sin, it is at least a suggestive image of how we can decide what counts as sin. If one does a socially acceptable thing (like taking a glass of wine for abstainers or a hamburger for vegetarians), and yet that socially acceptable thing violates one's own Christian faithfulness, that deed is sin. But perhaps there are larger implications, too. If one condemns another person, not out of the deep faith in the God who justifies the ungodly, but out of a kind of easy assumption that my standards are God's standards, my judgment is also sin. If we had to make a list of the deeds we performed and the judgments we made which were not based in our faith in Jesus Christ, the list might go on forever.

Paul calls us to the obedience of faith. That does not mean that "anything goes" for Christians, but it does mean that we are free to engage in a great many activities that really do not affect our faith one way or the other. It also means that we are called to be open to other people who may live very differently than we live, but who also are part of God's call, God's plan, God's justifying, God's welcome. When we refuse to welcome those whom God has welcomed, our self-righteousness is sin (like the older brother outside the party, missing the fun and missing the point as well).

Whatever does not come from faith is sin, and whatever comes from faith is *not* sin. One of the great gifts and challenges of understanding Paul is to try to find in our own time what distinguishes obedient faith from generally acceptable behavior, or doing what the neighbors do, or general good citizenship, or keeping up our race, class, and cultural prejudices.

Paul's reminder to us not to judge one another and not to cause the other to stumble remains continuingly helpful, even if the main issues in our time are not vegetarianism or fast days.

There are obviously issues that involve eating and drinking which divide Christians to this day, and what seems to one believer an exercise in Christian freedom, to another is a temptation to sin. Those who have one set of standards will not tempt others to violate their own standards.

There are other divisive issues as well. Churches are divided on issues of inclusive language. This book and others in this series are governed by the principle that our language about God and about other people should be as inclusive as possible, not limited by masculine nouns or pronouns. However, we have to admit that some imagery for God (God as Mother, for instance) seems to some Christians ground for stumbling, not just because they are picky and old-fashioned, but because theologically they believe that is a mistaken view of God. It is equally clear that always referring to God in masculine language provides a stumbling block to those for whom those words seem hopelessly oppressive.

Language is extremely important, but God is not the words we use about God, and even in cases of language, love is the greatest gift. What would Paul say about our disputes over words? What does it mean that whatever does not proceed from faith is sin?

Questions about appropriate sexuality and responsible behavior also can divide Christian from Christian. How can we avoid judging one another without simply giving up our own strong principles? What does it mean that all of us live and die to the Lord, that judgment is God's, and that in the meantime we are called to live together as Christ's body? Welcomed. Welcoming.

Christ Our Example
(Romans 15:1–6)

> 15:1 **We who are strong ought to put up with the failings of the weak, and not to please ourselves.** 2 **Each of us must please our neighbor for the good purpose of building up the neighbor.** 3 **For Christ did not please himself; but, as it is written, "The insults of those who insult you have fallen on me."** 4 **For whatever was written in former days was written for our instruction, so that by steadfastness and by the encouragement of the scriptures we might have hope.** 5 **May the God of steadfastness and encouragement grant you to live in harmony with one another, in accordance with Christ Jesus,** 6 **so that together you may with one voice glorify the God and Father of our Lord Jesus Christ.**

We have said that the whole theme of Romans 12—15 is the obedience of faith. We could equally well say that the whole theme of Romans 12—15 is right worship. Paul has told us that right worship requires that our bodies—our whole selves—work out what is acceptable to God through our obedience. Right worship is also the worship of all God's people: "so that together you may with one voice glorify the God and Father of our Lord Jesus Christ."

What Paul has heard of the Roman churches suggests that they are not of one voice but of many. They do not live together as God's people but in divisions. There are divisions between "strong" and "weak" in faith. There are divisions between Jewish Christians and Gentile Christians. Again he calls the Roman Christians to be who they are: one body in Jesus Christ.

Because they are Christ's body they are called to be who Christ was. In Romans 15:3, Paul quotes Psalm 69:9: "The insults of those who insult you have fallen on me." That is, for the sake of others Christ was willing to forgo his own rights, his own privileges, his own boasting. The Roman Christians are invited, reminded, to do the same.

The Romans are reminded to be who Christ was, because Paul quotes scripture to them, and the point of quoting scripture is to re-mind us, to bring our minds back to what we ought to know. Scripture provides information, but it is not simply facts that we get from scripture. We get encouragement and hope. Using the Bible to pile up facts and using the Bible to start arguments is very far from what Paul here has in mind. The Bible is a fountain of hope.

Of course, for Paul, scripture is our Old Testament. We have seen throughout Romans that Paul believes the Old Testament not only points to Jesus Christ but describes Jesus Christ. Our scripture includes more than Paul's scripture did. It includes Paul's letters and the Gospels and the other books of the New Testament. But what Paul saw in his scripture we see in the whole Bible: encouragement, hope.

In the light of scripture, the Romans are encouraged to get along with one another. To live out the life that Christ lived: "in harmony with one another, in accordance with Christ Jesus." (For a similar plea, see Phil. 2:1–11.)

When Paul wrote Romans, there were no denominations, but there were already divisions among churches. There was no split between so-called evangelicals and so-called liberals, but there were certainly divisions between the strong in faith and the weak. There were even divisions among the apostles, as a reading of Galatians will quickly show.

Differences may have their place in the body of Christ, but divisiveness does not. Divisiveness destroys hope and encourages boasting: my denomination has right doctrine and growing numbers; yours is mistaken and shrinking away. God has told me just how to understand scripture, and if you don't see it my way, you don't see it God's way. (Like the bumper sticker we see: "God said it. I believe it. That settles it.")

I do not know that Paul would be appalled to find churches of four different denominations at the busy corners of our cities and towns. I am quite sure he would be appalled if Christians from those different churches never came together to the dinner table or the Communion table.

Paul's hope would be that, encouraged by scripture, all Christian people could come together to sing with one voice a hymn to the one God, who through the one Lord Jesus Christ brings us to God's self in one way: through faith. True faith brings us together; false faiths drive us apart. True faith is in the God who unites; false faith is in the gods who divide, however orthodox the language with which we describe them.

Welcome in Christ
(Romans 15:7–13)

> 15:7 **Welcome one another, therefore, just as Christ has welcomed you, for the glory of God. [8] For I tell you that Christ has become a servant of the circumcised on behalf of the truth of God in order that he might confirm the promises given to the patriarchs, [9] and in order that the Gentiles might glorify God for his mercy. As it is written,**
>   **"Therefore I will confess you among the Gentiles,**
>   **and sing praises to your name";**
> [10] **and again he says,**
>   **"Rejoice, O Gentiles, with his people";**
> [11] **and again,**
>   **"Praise the Lord, all you Gentiles,**
>   **and let all the peoples praise him";**
> [12] **and again Isaiah says,**
>   **"The root of Jesse shall come,**
>   **the one who rises to rule the Gentiles;**
>   **in him the Gentiles shall hope."**
> [13] **May the God of hope fill you with all joy and peace in believing, so that you may abound in hope by the power of the Holy Spirit.**

Again, the main issue is the unity of the churches. Now the issue is addressed not as the division between the strong in faith and the weak in faith but as the division between Gentile and Jewish Christians. We have already suggested that there may be considerable overlap between "strong" Christians and Gentiles on the one hand and "weak" Christians and Jews on the other, but the identification is not complete. (Paul, the Jewish Christian, clearly considers himself strong in faith, for example.)

In Romans 1—8 Paul writes of how God's promises began with Israel, and especially with Abraham, and have been extended to the Gentiles. In Romans 9—11 Paul writes of how God's mercy in Jesus Christ has been received mostly by Gentiles, but it will soon be extended to most of Israel as well.

Now Paul writes mostly to the Gentile Christians in Rome to remind them that, apart from God's mercy to Israel, they would not have been included in God's family, in God's welcome. Because the Jews are the older brothers and sisters of the Gentiles in God's family, there is all the more reason for Gentiles to welcome the Jews.

Of course the reminder works both ways: "Welcome one another, just as Christ has welcomed you, for the glory of God." Christians are to welcome one another for the glory of God (so that they can praise God with one voice). Christ has welcomed all people for the glory of God. For the one God is glorified only when *all* people are welcomed into God's mercy.

The NRSV translates Romans 15:8–9a in this way: "For I tell you that Christ has become a servant of the circumcised on behalf of the truth of God in order that he might confirm the promises given to the patriarchs, and in order that the Gentiles mighty glorify God for his mercy." The Greek word for servant is *diakonos*, deacon or minister. However the word "deacon" quite often meant an emissary or representative of another. Notice how Paul speaks of his opponents as "deacons of Satan" for instance in 2 Corinthians 11:15, while he himself is a "deacon" of God, in 6:4. In 3:6, Paul is a deacon of the new covenant. In our own letter, in Romans 13:4, the authority is a "deacon" of God to keep order, a representative. (See John N. Collins, *Diakonia,* 227–28.)

Usually when people use the phrase "deacon of someone," by "someone" they mean the person or value they represent, not the person or value they serve; the one who sends them, not the one to whom they are sent. Paul as God's deacon doesn't just serve God, he represents God to the people. If this is correct, a more accurate translation of Romans 15:8–9a might be this: "For I tell you that Christ became a *representative from* the circumcised that he might confirm the promises given to the patriarchs, in order that the Gentiles might glorify God for his mercy." Paul has just been telling Gentile Roman Christians that God in Christ has welcomed them. Now he says, that, in so doing, Christ has served as a representative of the Jewish people, of the circumcised. Of course Jesus is first of all God's emissary, but he is also Israel's emissary to the Gentiles. Since in Christ, Israel's promise has been extended to the Gentiles, now surely Gentile Christians will welcome Jewish Christians as God in Christ (God's deacon) has welcomed them.

The list of quotations from the Old Testament shows that God has extended God's mercy from Israel to the Gentiles, but that mercy has begun with Israel and come to the Gentiles only at the last. All the more reason for the Gentiles, therefore, to welcome Israel. (It is as if we had yet one more scene in the story of the prodigal son. The prodigal, rejoicing at the party and devouring the fatted calf, is invited by the father to welcome the elder brother to the feast. Since all that belongs to the father belongs to the older brother, he too has been prepared a place at the feast from the beginning.)

Paul's first quotation here is from Psalm 18:49. In its context it combines praising God among the Gentiles, or nations, and thanking God for God's steadfast love to "David and his descendants forever" (Psalm 18:50). The second quotation, from Deuteronomy 32, is translated using different manuscripts in the NRSV's translation of the Old Testament, but in the version Paul quotes in Romans 15:10, what strikes us is the combination of praise among the Gentiles on the one hand and the people, Israel, on the other. Here indeed Paul sees God glorified with one voice. The quotation in Romans 15:11 is from Psalm 117:1, and it includes the same combination of the Gentiles and the people (Israel), joined in praise. The quotation in Romans 15:12 is from Isaiah 11. Jesus Christ is the root of Jesse. He is the one who brings the promises of Israel to the Gentiles. He does this so that all the people God created can praise the one God who created them. This Jew opens God's mercy to the Gentiles. Now surely, says Paul, the Gentile Christians in Rome will want to open their arms to their Jewish brothers and sisters: "Welcome one another, therefore, just as Christ has welcomed you, for the glory of God."

One way to talk about what God has done in Jesus Christ is for the church to declare God's welcome to every human being. There are no dues you have to pay to know God's love, no hoops to jump through to enter into God's presence, no steps to climb, no set of rules you have to obey before God's arms will open. God has run down the steps from the porch and down the road to welcome each one of us as we come home penitent from the far country, and to welcome every last one of our brothers and sisters, too.

After the quotations, Paul glorifies God with a benediction. It combines the themes we have seen in this section of Romans and throughout the letter. God is the God of hope; that hope is revealed to us in scripture and confirmed by the Spirit (see especially Romans 8). The way we lay hold of hope is through faith (NRSV "believing"; Rom. 15:13). The one who is in a right relationship to God will live through faith; the one who has a right relationship to God through faith will live—now and forever.

Faith is a gift to Jews and Gentiles alike. Through faith all are called to joy, and all are blessed with peace.

May the God of hope fill you with all joy and peace in believing, so that you
may abound in hope by the power of the Holy Spirit. (Rom. 15:13)

Now Paul is ready to move to his closing reminders, a definition of his
mission, and a recollection of his purpose in writing the letter. Much of
that purpose has just become clear. Paul writes to encourage the hope that
brings Christians together, to overcome the divisiveness that tears them
apart.

His word is still a word to us, so busily trying to find the claims and the
practices that can divide us, so that we can be reassured of our Reformed
heritage or our Anglican way or our Baptist distinctives. All well and good,
but not good enough. What is good enough is the mercy of God that welcomes us all to the party. What is good enough is the faithful obedience
by which we always reach out to welcome one another. What is good
enough is the hymn we sing together, with one voice to the one God who
has given us the one Lord, Jesus Christ.

6. Paul's Closing Reminders
Romans 15:14–16:27

The books of the New Testament have been passed down to us in many manuscripts. The differences among ancient manuscripts are often very slight, but the ancient manuscripts of Romans contain significant differences in the last chapter and a half of that letter.

Certain verses from Romans 15:14–16:27 appear in different places in different manuscripts, and some sections are missing altogether in some texts. For the most part, the place where we find a different verse or two does not make a huge difference in understanding Paul's letter. Because this book is an interpretation of the NRSV translation of the New Testament, and because the committee that translated the NRSV has made thoughtful decisions about what text to present, I have interpreted the text as it is printed in that translation.

One other issue emerges from the differences among these texts. Partly because of the variations in this last part of Romans in different manuscripts, some people have thought that chapter 16 was part of another letter and was added to Romans sometime after Paul wrote to the churches at Rome, perhaps to accompany the letter to churches elsewhere. This has seemed especially plausible because of the many people Paul names in Romans 16. Would he have known all these people in a community he had never visited?

I am convinced that our letter to the Romans was written for the Roman churches, from beginning to end. This makes the best sense of the different manuscripts. Further, the long list of names may make *better* sense if Paul has never visited the churches he is writing. He is assuring the Roman Christians that not only does he preach a real gospel but people they know and trust honor and recognize him. There was much travel in the Roman Empire of Paul's time, and it is not at all impossible that he writes to people he knew elsewhere in his travels. For instance, Acts 18:1–4 tells us that Paul met Priscilla and Aquila in Corinth, after they had been expelled from Rome. Now, when he writes Romans, they have returned.

REASONS AND HOPES
Romans 15:14–33

Why Paul Writes Boldly (Romans 15:14–21)

15:14 **I myself feel confident about you, my brothers and sisters, that you yourselves are full of goodness, filled with all knowledge, and able to instruct one another.** [15] **Nevertheless on some points I have written to you rather boldly by way of reminder, because of the grace given me by God** [16] **to be a minister of Christ Jesus to the Gentiles in the priestly service of the gospel of God, so that the offering of the Gentiles may be acceptable, sanctified by the Holy Spirit.** [17] **In Christ Jesus, then, I have reason to boast of my work for God.** [18] **For I will not venture to speak of anything except what Christ has accomplished through me to win obedience from the Gentiles, by word and deed,** [19] **by the power of signs and wonders, by the power of the Spirit of God, so that from Jerusalem and as far around as Illyricum I have fully proclaimed the good news of Christ.** [20] **Thus I make it my ambition to proclaim the good news, not where Christ has already been named, so that I do not build on someone else's foundation,** [21] **but as it is written,**
"Those who have never been told of him shall see,
and those who have never heard of him shall understand."

In these paragraphs, Paul explains both why he has not yet visited the Roman Christians and why he nonetheless makes bold to share with them the meaning of the gospel through this letter.

He has not visited them because his great mission is to proclaim the gospel to Gentiles who have never heard the gospel. Others have preached and started churches in Rome, so Paul's ministry has not been needed there. He has been bold to write to them because his great mission is to proclaim the gospel to *Gentiles*. God has called Paul to be God's missionary to the Gentiles, and God's Spirit has confirmed that call because Paul has done signs and wonders among the Gentiles. We do not know exactly what signs and wonders Paul has done, but clearly part of his ministry included miraculous deeds. These were not really *his* deeds but were the work of the Holy Spirit, confirming Paul's ministry in this way. (See also 2 Cor. 12:12.)

What Paul seeks to bring about through this ministry is "the obedience of the Gentiles"—that concern with which our letter began. Faith is worked out in obedience. Perhaps Paul here tips his hand that his particular concern in writing this letter is to persuade the Gentiles to be more open to Jewish Christians and supportive of differences within the churches. He wants them to be more obedient to the implications of the gospel.

The phrase in verse 18, "by word and deed," can be interpreted in two ways. It can mean that by his words and deeds Paul has evoked obedience from the Gentiles. It can mean that Paul has evoked from the Gentiles their obedience in both word and deed. Perhaps it means both these things. Paul's faithful obedience includes word and deed; the faithful obedience of Gentile Christians includes both word and deed as well.

Paul thinks of his ministry to the Gentiles as a priestly ministry, like that of the high priest of the Old Testament, who brings offerings to God. The offering Paul brings is the offering of the Gentiles. That means that the Gentiles *are* an offering; their lives (as in Romans 12:1) are a living sacrifice, holy and acceptable. It also means that the Gentiles are invited to provide an offering—the gift for the relief of the saints in Jerusalem. Paul now turns to that topic as well.

A Visit to Rome, a Visit to Jerusalem
(Romans 15:22–33)

15:22 **This is the reason that I have so often been hindered from coming to you.** [23] **But now, with no further place for me in these regions, I desire, as I have for many years, to come to you** [24] **when I go to Spain. For I do hope to see you on my journey and to be sent on by you, once I have enjoyed your company for a little while.** [25] **At present, however, I am going to Jerusalem in a ministry to the saints;** [26] **for Macedonia and Achaia have been pleased to share their resources with the poor among the saints at Jerusalem.** [27] **They were pleased to do this, and indeed they owe it to them; for if the Gentiles have come to share in their spiritual blessings, they ought also to be of service to them in material things.** [28] **So, when I have completed this, and have delivered to them what has been collected, I will set out by way of you to Spain;** [29] **and I know that when I come to you, I will come in the fullness of the blessing of Christ.**

[30] **I appeal to you, brothers and sisters, by our Lord Jesus Christ and by the love of the Spirit, to join me in earnest prayer to God on my behalf,** [31] **that I may be rescued from the unbelievers in Judea, and that my ministry to Jerusalem may be acceptable to the saints,** [32] **so that by God's will I may come to you with joy and be refreshed in your company.** [33] **The God of peace be with all of you. Amen.**

In at least three ways Paul is deeply concerned with the relationship of Jews to Gentiles in God's plan to redeem the world and in the ongoing life of the church. He is concerned with the relationship of Jews to Gentiles because of his deep faith that God wants a right relationship with all people—Jews first, but Gentiles as well. He is concerned with this relationship because the churches at Rome apparently are experiencing some friction between Jewish Christians and Gentile Christians. He is concerned with this relationship because his hope and prayer is that his own ministry to the Gentiles will be acknowledged and accepted by the Jewish Christians who are in Jerusalem.

The offering that Paul has collected in Macedonia and Achaia is a sign of the concern of the Gentiles for Jewish Christians in need. It is also a sign of the unity of the church. As the Jews have shared the spiritual blessings they have inherited with Gentiles, so now the Gentiles are sharing material blessings, goods, with Jewish Christians. When the Jerusalem church accepts the Gentile offerings, they will also acknowledge Paul's ministry and his place as a real apostle, called by Christ as surely as Peter and James were called.

Paul is clearly concerned that unbelievers may block his attempt to present the offering in Jerusalem, but he is even more concerned that believers may refuse to accept that offering. There is considerable evidence elsewhere in the New Testament (perhaps especially in Galatians) that Paul did not always have an easy time persuading other Christians and other Christian leaders of his own mission as an apostle. The difficulty that Roman Christians apparently have in accepting one another is a difficulty that had affected Paul's own ministry. Some Jewish Christians doubted that Paul's gospel to Gentile Christians gave enough credit to the importance of the law for believing people. When Paul writes to the Romans about the one God who justifies all people through faith and not through the law, he reflects in part a long struggle in his own ministry to persuade law-abiding Jewish Christians that his interpretation of the gospel is valid.

Of course, Paul's three concerns about the relationship of Jews to Gentiles go together. Paul tells the Romans about God's plan to redeem all of humankind in part to encourage them to be more welcoming to one another. He may also encourage them to be more welcoming to one another so that Jewish Christians in Rome will encourage Jewish Christians in Jerusalem to acknowledge Paul as a true apostle and to welcome the offering as he intends it—as a sign of the church's unity. If we are right that the long list of names in Romans 16 represents people Paul had met in his travels who were now living in Rome, we can guess that this Christian commerce went both ways. Jewish Christians from elsewhere may well visit Jerusalem from time to time, or may send letters to Jerusalem Christians, and their support might help Paul win the acceptance he so eagerly desires.

When we read Paul, we think so clearly of his zeal for the gospel that we may forget that that zeal includes a profound love for the church and a profound desire that the church find its own unity. His ministry becomes a sign to the churches of our own day that all of us have spiritual blessings to give and to receive. If each congregation is Christ's body and each Christian a member, so too the universal church is Christ's worldwide body. Different denominations, different congregations, different theological biases represent interdependent parts of a whole people, a whole family.

Today, the ecumenical movement seems to have lost some of its steam as we move toward the end of the century, and perhaps the enthusiasm for new structures was bound to wane. Paul's gospel, however, continually pushes us toward a vision of Christianity that encompasses us all. All of us are always bringing offerings to one another, and receiving others' gifts in return.

In particular, so-called mainline churches look askance at what seems the naïveté of so-called evangelical churches, while evangelical churches often accuse mainliners of selling out to the devices and desires of the secular world. Yet, just as the early church needed both evangelists and prophets, so the contemporary church needs the zeal to win new members and the zeal to understand the church in the light of our own times and our own culture (as Paul continually interpreted scripture in the light of his time and culture). If we can stop yelling at each other and start learning from each other, we will discover that the God of peace is still at work among us.

Surely Paul's invocation of the God of peace at this point in his letter is entirely appropriate. Recall that he first greets the Roman Christians with the greeting "Grace to you and peace from God our Father and the Lord Jesus Christ" (Rom. 1:7b). The great claim of the letter has been that all of us come to God through the grace of Jesus Christ, the free gift that brings us into a right relationship with God. When we are in a right relationship with God we also live in peace—Jews and Gentiles in the Roman churches; Jews and Gentiles in the church throughout the world; the Jewish Christian leaders and Paul as apostle to the Gentiles. Looking at Paul's words for today, we still invoke the God of peace to bring us together—Catholics, Orthodox, and Protestants; Christians of different races, languages, and theological convictions.

The failure of peace in the church today is a direct result of the weakening of faith. Had we the faith to know that our redemption is always grace, gift, mercy, we would not think it necessary to parade our credentials, to show how much we've earned in our attempt to please God. We would not boast that we are more zealous for social justice than the Christians in the next block, or love the Bible more, or preserve family values more faithfully, or alone know how to celebrate the sacraments. Whatever does not proceed from faith is sin, and whatever injures peace does not proceed from faith. Paul, who knew how to stir up a fuss, was usually fussing at Christians to stop fussing at one another. His prayer still counts: "The God of peace be with all of you."

PERSONAL GREETINGS
Romans 16:1–16

16:1 I commend to you our sister Phoebe, a deacon of the church at Cenchreae, [2] so that you may welcome her in the Lord as is fitting for the saints, and help her in whatever she may require from you, for she has been a benefactor of many and of myself as well.

[3] Greet Prisca and Aquila, who work with me in Christ Jesus, [4] and who risked their necks for my life, to whom not only I give thanks, but also all the churches of the Gentiles. [5] Greet also the church in their house. Greet my beloved Epaenetus, who was the first convert in Asia for Christ. [6] Greet Mary, who has worked very hard among you. [7] Greet Andronicus and Junia, my relatives who were in prison with me; they are prominent among the apostles, and they were in Christ before I was. [8] Greet Ampliatus, my beloved in the Lord. [9] Greet Urbanus, our co-worker in Christ, and my beloved Stachys. [10] Greet Apelles, who is approved in Christ. Greet those who belong to the family of Aristobulus. [11] Greet my relative Herodion. Greet those in the Lord who belong to the family of Narcissus. [12] Greet those workers in the Lord, Tryphaena and Tryphosa. Greet the beloved Persis, who has worked hard in the Lord. [13] Greet Rufus, chosen in the Lord; and greet his mother—a mother to me also. [14] Greet Asyncritus, Phlegon, Hermes, Patrobas, Hermas, and the brothers and sisters who are with them. [15] Greet Philologus, Julia, Nereus and his sister, and Olympas, and all the saints who are with them. [16] Greet one another with a holy kiss. All the churches of Christ greet you.

This long list of greetings in fact provides some interesting clues to the early Christian communities at Rome. There is a great mix in the list—of names that are presumably Jewish in origin and those that are Gentile— some Greek and some probably Roman and Latin. Paul greets with affection as fellow believers both men and women, with no sense that one group is more important than the other.

Peter Lampe points out that the mention of those Roman Christians who are Paul's family or compatriots (Andronicus, Junia, and Herodion) underlines Paul's claim in Romans 11:1–6 that a remnant of the Jewish people have accepted Christ. Here is a brief list of some Jews who have come to believe. When we combine this list with Paul's inclusion of himself in the remnant in Romans 11, we can see that the presence of Jewish Christians among Paul's faithful friends is a sign of God's continuing relationship to the Jewish people. The greetings to these Jewish Christians may also strengthen Paul's reminder to the Roman Gentile Christians to welcome the Jewish Christians in their midst. (See Lampe, in *The Romans Debate*, 224–25.)

Phoebe, whom Paul commends to the Christians at Rome, is designated as a *diakonos*. This Greek word often means "minister," even as Paul applies it to himself (see, for instance, 1 Cor. 3:5 and 2 Cor. 3:6; 6:4, 11:23). Clearly Phoebe has a role of some importance in the early community, and "minister" is probably a better translation than "deacon." Sometimes a "minister," or *diakonos*, is a person who carries out a commission from another. (In 2 Cor. 11:15, Paul refers to false apostles as "deacons" or "emissaries" from Satan.) Phoebe may be Christ's emissary in the church at Cenchreae, as Paul has been Christ's emissary in Corinth. In Philippians 1:1, "deacons" are apparently local church leaders, though they may not yet be officers in any institutionalized way. Older translations sometimes called Phoebe a "deaconess," but the Greek word gives no reason to think that she has a leadership role reserved for women. She is a "deacon" or "minister."

The greeting to Prisca and Aquila (Rom. 16:3) reinforces claims we have already made about the situation of the Roman church. The churches were relatively small communities meeting in homes, and one church in Rome meets in Prisca and Aquila's home. Romans 16:14 and 16:15, with their references to Christians who are "with" other Christians, may also give evidence for groups of Christians meeting in homes. Furthermore, the claim that both Paul and all the churches of the Gentiles give thanks for these two Jewish Christians (see Acts 18:1–2) is a not-too-subtle reminder to Gentile Christians in Rome that they, too, should welcome Prisca and Aquila home and should welcome their house church to fellowship with Gentile Christians. This is clearly an attempt to establish authority by association. Paul wants to strengthen Prisca and Aquila in their relationship to the Gentile Christians and presumably hopes that their enhanced authority in Rome may help enhance his own. (Prisca here is certainly the same person as Priscilla in Acts 18:3. The different English forms represent different forms of the same name in the original Greek texts.)

Notice, too, that Junia and Andronicus are counted among the apostles (Rom. 16:7). This suggests two features of the churches Paul knows. First, for Paul, the apostles are not just the twelve people we usually think of as apostles (though that is how they are designated in the book of Acts), or even the twelve plus Paul. For Paul there are other apostles, and all we know is their names. Perhaps there were other apostles whose names are now lost to history. Second, Junia is almost certainly a woman, so there is not only a woman known to the Romans whom Paul calls a minister, there is a woman known to the Romans whom Paul calls an apostle.

If it turns out that Paul knew both ministers and apostles who were women, it becomes very difficult for contemporary churches to insist that women should not be ordained as ministers or bishops, as if that were a way to uphold the earliest practice of the church. Although there may be reasons for refusing to ordain women, my own conviction is that there are not any good reasons. The earliest testimony to the practice of the first-century church suggests that opponents of women's ordination will not find the evidence they want in these sources.

Notice how often Paul refers to the believers in Rome as people who are "in Christ" or "in the Lord." Paul's word for someone we would call "Christian" is someone who is "in Christ." Everything we have seen about the importance of baptism and about Paul's strong belief that Christians are members of Christ's body shows that this isn't just a catch phrase. It is a profound understanding of Christian identity. To whom do you belong? In whose sphere is your life and its meaning? Are you in Christ or in sin? In Christ or in the law? In Christ or in death?

What we get is a picture of a quite diverse church community and a community of Christians often on the move. These are probably neither the poorest nor the wealthiest people in Rome; they are both Jews and Gentiles, both men and women. They are united by the fact that, like Paul, they are "in Christ." Paul stresses their unity with one another, their unity with him, and their unity with Christians in all the other churches he knows. *The* church is bigger than the house church in Prisca and Aquila's home, bigger than the communities of Jewish Christians or Gentile Christians, bigger than the whole Christian community in Rome. The church encompasses the world from east to west and is a foreshadowing of the day when all the creation will rejoice in the revealing of the children of God. If Paul succeeds in passing through Rome and going to Spain, he will have preached the gospel from east to west in the known world, and in the world's capital city, too. His ministry will be a further sign of God's intention to bring all of humankind into a right relationship with God's own self and with one another.

Perhaps most important, when Paul urges the Roman Christians to greet all these believers whom Paul knows, he reminds them that he himself is a Christian of no mean importance. They are to pay attention to this list of his friends and, by implication, they are to pay attention to Paul as well. They are to welcome all these distinguished Christians who know him, and in God's own time they will also welcome Paul as he stops at Rome on his way to Spain. And they will welcome this letter, from a Christian who is both Christ's servant and apostle, and who knows hard-working Mary; is related to Adronicus, Junia, and Herodion; knows Apelles, whom Christ approves; and loves Rufus's mother as if she were his own.

Finally, when Paul tells the Roman Christians that "all the churches of Christ greet you," he suggests their unity with a community larger than their confederation of house churches. And again, he stresses his own authority as one who is called by God to speak for all the churches, from east to west.

FINAL WARNING, FINAL BLESSING
Romans 16:17–27

16:17 **I urge you, brothers and sisters, to keep an eye on those who cause dissensions and offenses, in opposition to the teaching that you have learned; avoid them. [18] For such people do not serve our Lord Christ, but their own appetites, and by smooth talk and flattery they deceive the hearts of the simple-minded. [19] For while your obedience is known to all, so that I rejoice over you, I want you to be wise in what is good and guileless in what is evil. [20] The God of peace will shortly crush Satan under your feet. The grace of our Lord Jesus Christ be with you.**

[21]Timothy, my co-worker, greets you; so do Lucius and Jason and Sosipater, my relatives.

[22]I, Tertius, the writer of this letter, greet you in the Lord.

[23]Gaius, who is host to me and to the whole church, greets you. Erastus, the city treasurer, and our brother Quartus, greet you.

[Some versions include another doxology here as verse 24: The grace of our Lord Jesus Christ be with all of you. Amen.]

[25]Now to God who is able to strengthen you according to my gospel and the proclamation of Jesus Christ, according to the revelation of the mystery that was kept secret for long ages [26]but is now disclosed, and through the prophetic writings is made known to all the Gentiles, according to the command of the eternal God, to bring about the obedience of faith—[27]to the only wise God, through Jesus Christ, to whom be the glory forever! Amen.

No one knows what troublemakers Paul is so concerned about in the first part of this section. In passing, he has mentioned people who accuse him of advocating doing evil that good may come of it (Rom. 3:8), but there is little sense that this is a grave concern for him in his advice to the Romans. Certainly here he is not worrying about the relationships between Jewish and Gentile Christians, since he has assumed all along that people from both groups intend to live out their faith with goodwill. If we continue to assume that chapter 16 was an original part of the letter to the Romans, then Paul here responds in closing to some situation that worries him, but about which we have no real clues at all. It's a little like those letters we send our children or receive from our parents. After discussing the major concerns of our lives the letters end with a quick list of warnings: "Don't forget to take your medicine." Or "I told you not to date so-and-so." These are not the main things we parents want to talk about, but as long as we have your attention, we sign off by listing our worries, so that we can go on to our farewell, our blessing. Love, Mother. Love, Father. Peace.

We also note that for Paul, the God of peace does not provide peace for those who would work havoc in the church. The God of peace will bring peace by silencing troublemakers.

Of course, one difficult issue for the church, from Paul's day to our own, is the issue of discerning who is really a threat to the church's unity and who is simply a dissenter or a bother. Everything we have seen suggests that Paul is generous in the diversity he prays for in the church, but there are discernible outer limits. Perhaps he worries particularly about those whose view of Christian charity is less encompassing and compassionate than his own, but in these verses we cannot know that for sure.

Verses 21–23 remind us that even the apostle did not minister alone. He is aided by co-workers and relatives. He depends on the hospitality of Gaius and others. He dictates his letter to Tertius. Paul insists in Romans 12 that the church is a body whose different members have different responsibilities. His own ministry is fulfilled in cooperation with many others.

Many students have thought that the final blessing in our edition of Romans (Rom. 15:25–27) was written by someone later than Paul, perhaps when the letter was included in a collection of letters. The language sometimes sounds more like one of Paul's followers than like Paul himself. If so, the disciple has caught several of Paul's themes. God's goodness, revealed in the scripture—our Old Testament—has reached out beyond Israel to include the Gentiles, too. Paul's hope is that Gentiles (and of course the Jews, before them and after them) will come to faith and to the obedience that faith includes. And all of this, God's bringing us to God's self, our faithful obedience, all of this happens to the glory of God—forever.

The one God who brought Israel to God's self now brings the Gentiles, too, through the one Lord, Jesus Christ. All people accept God's goodness through faith. The faith of all God's people glorifies the God who created all and wills to redeem the whole creation.

We, too, after all these years, read these words and discover what is really gospel, good news. God chooses to be our God through Jesus Christ, and nothing in heaven or on earth can separate us from God's love. That is Paul's message to us as it was to the Romans, with the hope that in all our oddity and diversity, we may welcome one another as Christ has already welcomed us—for the glory of God.

Works Cited

Achtemeier, Paul J. *Romans*. Interpretation: A Bible Commentary for Teaching and Preaching. Atlanta: John Knox Press, 1985.

Barth, Karl. *The Epistle to the Romans*, trans. Edwyn C. Hoskyns. Oxford: Oxford University Press, 1977 (first published 1933).

Bethge, Eberhard. *Dietrich Bonhoeffer: Man of Vision, Man of Courage*, trans. Eric Mosbacher et al. New York: Harper & Row, 1977 (English translation first published 1970).

Collins, John N., *Diakonia: Re-interpreting the Ancient Sources*. New York: Oxford University Press, 1990.

Hays, Richard. *The Faith of Jesus Christ: An Investigation of the Narrative Substructure of Galatians 3:1–4:11*. Chico, Calif.: Scholars Press, 1983.

Hopkins, Gerard Manley. *Poems of Gerard Manley Hopkins*. New York and London: Oxford University Press, 1948.

Lampe, Peter. "The Roman Christians of Romans 16," in *The Romans Debate*, ed. Karl Donfried, 216–30. Peabody, Mass.: Hendrickson Publishers, 1991.

Luther, Martin. *A Brief Instruction on What to Look for and Expect in the Gospels*, trans. E. Theodore Bachmann, in Richard Lischer, *Theories of Preaching: Selected Readings in the Homiletical Tradition*, 95–99. Durham, N.C.: Labyrinth Press, 1987. (From *Luther's Works*, vol. 35, ed. E. Theodore Bachmann and Helmut Lehmann, 117–23; Philadelphia: Fortress Press, 1970.)

———. *Luther: Lectures on Romans*, trans. and ed. Wilhelm Pauck. Library of Christian Classics. Philadelphia: Westminster Press, 1961.

Schubert, Paul. *The Form and Function of Pauline Thanksgivings*. Berlin: A. Töpelmann, 1939.

Scroggs, Robin. *The New Testament and Homosexuality: Contextual Background for Contemporary Debate*. Philadelphia: Fortress Press, 1983.

The hymn "Amazing Grace—How Sweet the Sound" is by John Newton, 1779, and is found in *The Presbyterian Hymnal*, 280. Louisville: Westminster/John Knox Press, 1990.

The hymn "When I Survey the Wondrous Cross" is by Isaac Watts, 1707, and is found in *The Presbyterian Hymnal*, 100–101. Louisville: Westminster/John Knox Press, 1990.

The hymn "Have Thine Own Way, Lord!" is by Adelaide A. Pollard, 1902, and is found in *The United Methodist Hymnal*, 382. Nashville: United Methodist Publishing House, 1989.

For Further Reading

Achtemeier, Paul J. *Romans.* Interpretation: A Bible Commentary for Teaching and Preaching. Atlanta: John Knox Press, 1985.

Barth, Karl, *The Epistle to the Romans,* trans. Edwyn C. Hoskyns. Oxford: Oxford University Press, 1977 (first published 1933).

Donfried, Karl P., ed. *The Romans Debate.* Peabody, Mass.: Hendrickson Publishers, 1991.

Käsemann, Ernst. *Commentary on Romans,* trans. G. W. Bromiley. Grand Rapids: Wm. B. Eerdmans Publishing Co., 1980.

Nygren, Anders. *Commentary on Romans.* Philadelphia: Fortress Press, 1949.

Stendahl, Krister. *Paul among the Jews and Gentiles.* Philadelphia: Fortress Press, 1976.

Stuhlmacher, Peter. *Paul's Letter to the Romans.* Trans. Scott J. Hafemann. Louisville: Westminster/John Knox Press, 1994.

Printed in the United States
25574LVS00004B/261

9 780664 252540